Senior Editor Scarlett O'Hara
Senior Designer Sheila Collins
Project Editor Ruth O'Rourke
US Editor Margaret Parrish
Designers Mik Gates, Dave Ball
Illustration Sheila Collins, Mik Gates, Simon Mumford

Managing Editor Francesca Baines
Managing Art Editor Phil Letsu
Publisher Andrew Macintyre
Publishing Director Jonathan Metcalf
Associate Publishing Director Liz Wheeler
Art Director Karen Self
Pre-Production Producer Gillian Reid
Senior Producer Vivienne Yong, Gary Batchelor
Jacket Editor Claire Gell
Jacket Designer Mark Cavanagh

First American Edition, 2016
Published in the United States by DK Publishing,
345 Hudson Street, New York, New York 10014

Copyright © 2016 Dorling Kindersley Limited
DK, a Division of Penguin Random House LLC
16 17 18 19 20   10 9 8 7 6 5 4 3 2 1
001 – 282999 – Jan17

A catalog record for this book is available from the Library of Congress.
ISBN 978-1-4654-5626-7

DK books are available at special discounts when purchased in bulk for sales
promotions, premiums, fund-raising, or educational use. For details, contact:
DK Publishing Special Markets, 345 Hudson Street, New York, New York 10014
SpecialSales@dk.com

Printed and bound in China.

A WORLD OF IDEAS:
SEE ALL THERE IS TO KNOW
www.dk.com

HEADS UP MONEY

WRITTEN BY
MARCUS WEEKS

CONSULTANT
DEREK BRADDON

Contents

06 A World of MONEY

08 What do ECONOMISTS DO?

Show me the MONEY

12 What is MONEY?

14 On the MARKET

16 Keeping up with CURRENCY

18 Fair EXCHANGE

20 Where did the MONEY go?

22 In Focus:
CRYPTOCURRENCIES

24 Making sence of
ECONOMICS

26 Money and economics
IN PRACTICE

What's it WORTH?

30 The ECONOMIC
Problem

32 Who gets WHAT?

34 In Focus:
ETHICAL TRADE

36 GOODS and SERVICES

38 SUPPLY and DEMAND

40 Why are some things
more VALUABLE?

42 A hive of INDUSTRY

44 In Focus:
PUBLIC COMPANIES

46 Healthy COMPETITION?

48 Who's in CHARGE?

50 How BUSINESSES operate

52 Running an EFFICIENT
business

54 In Focus: COOPERATIVE
MOVEMENTS

56 Going to WORK

58 BIG spenders

60 Resources and businesses
IN PRACTICE

Does money make the WORLD GO ROUND?

64 Let well enough ALONE

66 Free TRADE

68 It's a SMALL World

70 Economic UPS and DOWNS

72 In Focus: ECONOMIC BUBBLES

74 When markets don't DO THEIR JOB

76 A taxing PROBLEM

78 What does the FUTURE hold?

80 A RISKY business

82 An informed GAMBLE

84 In Focus: Hyperinflation

86 Is greed GOOD?

88 Making the RIGHT decision

90 In Focus: FINANCIAL CRISIS OF 2007-8

92 Costing the EARTH

94 Markets and trade IN PRACTICE

Can money buy HAPPINESS?

98 Measuring a country's WEALTH

100 Who's providing the MONEY?

102 Making MONEY out of thin air

104 Why are some countries POOR?

106 In Focus: INTERNATIONAL FINANCIAL INSTITUTIONS

108 Who benefits from GLOBALIZATION?

110 The POVERTY problem

112 Helping the DEVELOPING WORLD

114 In Focus: PROVIDING ENERGY

116 PAYBACK time!

118 The WAGE gap

120 Living standards and inequality IN PRACTICE

What's in my POCKET?

124 Finding a BALANCE

126 Earning a LIVING

128 A SAFE place for my money

130 Do you REALLY need that?

132 Looking after the PENNIES

134 Buy now, pay LATER?

136 In Focus: THE RATE FOR THE JOB

138 How would you like to PAY?

140 Travel MONEY

142 For a RAINY day...

144 Making PLANS

146 Personal finances IN PRACTICE

148 Directory of economists

152 Glossary

156 Index and Acknowledgments

A world of **MONEY**

IT HAS BEEN SAID THAT "MONEY MAKES THE WORLD GO ROUND" AND IT SEEMS THAT WE REALLY CAN'T LIVE WITHOUT IT. WE ALL NEED MONEY, AND YET FEW OF US REALLY UNDERSTAND WHAT MONEY IS AND WHY IT MATTERS SO MUCH. WHY DOES PAPER CURRENCY, A COIN, OR A PIECE OF PLASTIC ENABLE US TO BUY THE THINGS WE WANT? HOW DOES ECONOMICS AFFECT BUSINESSES AND JOBS? HOW DOES ECONOMICS AFFECT OUR ENVIRONMENT, OUR SOCIETY, AND THE WORLD? AND WHAT CHOICES DO WE NEED TO CONSIDER TO HAVE THE LIFE WE WANT AND TO SECURE OUR FUTURE?

Without money, we would have no choice but to barter and exchange things every day. How time-consuming and inefficient would this be? The invention of money as a means of exchange makes the economy function quickly and efficiently and enables us to conduct business on a global scale. Sterling was first introduced as currency in England in the reign of King Offa of Mercia (757—796 AD), with 240 silver pennies equaling one pound weight of silver, hence the pound sterling name. The United States adopted the dollar as the unit of currency in 1785, with a value of 270 grains of gold or 416 grains of silver. Once paper currencies became universally acceptable, gold and silver backing for a currency was ended and paper (or *fiat*) money became the norm.

Our economy today relies on *fiat* money, supplemented with additional forms of payment, such as credit cards, debit cards, prepaid cards, and, contactless payments via mobile phones.

Money also acts as a measure of value, a store of value (in the form of savings), and it can be used to transfer value between individuals. Money now no longer just facilitates trade—it has become a major world trading item in its own right for speculative reasons. The exchange of money through the world's money markets now exceeds $5 trillion every day. Less than 1% of this is associated with real trade; the other 99% is trade in money itself! Economics affects our lives in many ways, underpinning the industries we work for and the way our government operates, filtering through to the money in our wallets and how we spend it.

What do
ECONOMISTS DO?

ACADEMIC ECONOMISTS

Economics is taught in most schools and universities, and is a popular choice of subject for students looking forward to a career in business, finance, or government.

Teaching economics

Many economics students continue their studies at university, and some of these go on to become academic economists, teaching and researching economic theory.

Research economist

PUBLIC SECTOR ECONOMISTS

There are many career options in politics for economics students. Many politicians have studied economics, and governments employ professional economists to advise on policy.

Political economist

Many government departments employ people qualified in economics—tax and finance departments, for example. All branches of the civil service require economists.

Economists in government

PRIVATE SECTOR ECONOMISTS

Economics graduates work in banking. Either in consumer banks dealing with individuals and small businesses or in investment banks providing finance for larger corporations.

Banking

Studying economics is useful for traders in the financial markets, such as the stock exchange or commodities markets. Economists also work as analysts and advisers to trading firms.

Traders and analysts

ECONOMICS EXAMINES THE DIFFERENT WAYS THAT GOVERNMENTS, BUSINESSES, AND INDIVIDUALS MANAGE RESOURCES AND PROVIDE GOODS AND SERVICES. SOME PEOPLE WHO HAVE STUDIED ECONOMICS WORK AS ECONOMISTS, FOR EXAMPLE, AS ECONOMIC ADVISERS TO GOVERNMENTS OR BUSINESSES, OR THEY WORK IN A UNIVERSITY ECONOMICS DEPARTMENT. MANY MORE USE THEIR KNOWLEDGE OF ECONOMICS MORE INDIRECTLY IN OTHER CAREERS, IN BOTH THE PUBLIC AND PRIVATE SECTORS.

There are two main fields of economic study: macroeconomics and microeconomics. In macroeconomics the economies of countries and their governments are studied.

Macroeconomics

Microeconomics looks at specific aspects of the economy and examines the economic behavior of individuals and businesses buying and selling goods and services.

... and microeconomics

Students of economics often study subjects connected to economic ideas, such as business studies, politics, law, and sociology, but also subjects such as philosophy.

Applied economics

Economists may work in major international organizations, such as the UN and World Bank. Those specializing in development economics can also work for aid agencies and charities.

Development economics

Some economists work as accountants or financial advisers, guiding businesses, insurance firms, or individuals, on issues with savings, tax, and investments.

Financial advisers and accountants

TV, radio, and newspapers often employ a number of journalists with qualifications in economics to report on current affairs and offer an analysis of the news.

In the news

Show me the MONEY

What is MONEY?

On the MARKET

Keeping up with CURRENCY

Money plays an important part in all our lives. We earn money to buy the things we need, and to save for the future. We exchange our money for goods and services that are produced by all kinds of businesses. Economics is the subject that studies not just money, but the way that these goods and services are produced and managed.

Fair EXCHANGE

Where did the MONEY go?

Making SENSE of economics

What is **MONEY**?

MONEY PLAYS AN IMPORTANT PART IN ALL OUR LIVES. WE WORK HARD TO EARN IT, AND SOME PEOPLE TAKE HUGE RISKS TO GET MORE OF IT. SOMETIMES, WE JUDGE HOW SUCCESSFUL PEOPLE ARE BY HOW MUCH MONEY THEY HAVE, AND THERE ARE PEOPLE WHO SUFFER BECAUSE THEY DON'T HAVE ENOUGH OF IT.

Money, money, money

What exactly is money? When we think about money, most of us think of the cash—the bills and coins—we have in our pocket or wallet. But there's also money that is less obvious. You may, for example, get a check through the mail as a present from a relative, or a gift card to spend at a particular store. It's likely that you'll have a bank account where you keep most of your money, but never see it except as a number on your monthly statement. There are also credit and debit cards and ways of paying for things online, all of which require money.

Let's swap!

Money can take various forms, but the forms all have certain things in common. The first and most obvious is that we can buy things with it. It is what economists call a "medium of exchange." If someone is offering something that we want or need, we can offer them something we have in exchange. For example, a friend may have tickets to a baseball game that she doesn't want, and I offer to swap them for an extra set of headphones I have. Alternatively, I could sell the headphones to someone else, and use the money to buy the tickets from her. The money I am paid for the headphones is more useful to me, because I can use it to buy all kinds of things, and from many different people who may not want headphones.

...FOR MEASURING WORTH...

MONEY IS USED FOR SAVINGS...

MONEY PLAYS THE LARGEST PART IN DETERMINING THE COURSE OF HISTORY.
THE COMMUNIST MANIFESTO

⬆ What's the use?

Money has three main uses: storing value or saving, as a common unit for measuring what something is worth, and as a medium of exchange for buying goods or services.

... AND IN EXCHANGE FOR THINGS.

THE LOVE OF MONEY IS THE ROOT OF ALL EVIL.

KING JAMES BIBLE

See also: 22–23, 102–103

Lasting value

There is a third important function of money. It is a way of saving for the future, or as economists call it a "store of value." When we go to work, we get paid for what we do. If there were no money, we might be paid with things such as food or other necessities. However, if we receive a paycheck of money—or money is put into a bank account—it can be used to buy our food, clothes, and pay our bills; it can be used for many different things. If there is money left over after we have bought the things we need, it can be saved to be used later. There are other ways of storing value, for example, in artworks, property, or land, but money is far more flexible and easier to exchange. To be useful in this way, money must hold its value over time, so the money in our bank accounts can be used in exchange when it is needed.

Numismatics is the study or collection of money, such as in the form of coins and banknotes.

Putting a price on it

The question remains about how much the tickets, or the headphones, are worth. It's difficult to see if an exchange of two very different things is fair, unless we have a means of measuring the worth of the two items. This is another function of money: it is a way of putting a price on things, it works as what is known as a "unit of account." Money is a system of units, in much the same way that currencies like dollars, pounds, euros, or yen are. We can use these units to put a price on things and this allows us to compare their worth.

DOES MONEY HAVE A VALUE?

Imagine that you've been shipwrecked on a desert island. Washed up on the beach from the wreckage are: a suitcase crammed with cash, a wooden chest full of gold, and a crate of cans and packages of food. Which is most valuable to you? Are the money or the gold worth anything if you have nowhere to spend them?

On the **MARKET**

MOST PEOPLE THINK OF A MARKET AS A PLACE WHERE TRADERS SET UP STALLS TO SELL THEIR FRUIT, VEGETABLES, AND OTHER EVERYDAY ITEMS, OR PERHAPS THE MODERN SUPERMARKET OR SHOPPING MALL. BUT WHEN ECONOMISTS TALK OF "THE MARKET" IT HAS A WIDER MEANING, TO INCLUDE THE EXCHANGE OF ALL KINDS OF GOODS AND SERVICES.

> In ancient Greece, the marketplace, or *agora*, was also the social and political center of the city.

Getting what we need

In economics, the market is not a place, but the way in which we can get the things we need, such as our food, clothes, and appliances. It is also the way that producers of these things can offer them to us for sale. A producer of bicycles, for example, could put them up for sale on a market stall, but is more likely to sell them in stores and over the internet—these are different ways of putting them "on the market."

Markets began when people came to a particular place, the marketplace, to buy and sell things. At the stalls, sellers

◉ Goods and services

Providers of all kinds of goods and services sell their products by offering them on the market. Buyers can choose from a range of often connected commodities, manufactured goods, and services.

> **SUPPLY** ALWAYS COMES ON THE HEELS OF **DEMAND.**
> ROBERT COLLIER, SELF-HELP AUTHOR

offered goods—things they had produced, such as food—or services—things that they could do, such as cutting hair. In modern towns and cities, traditional markets are less common and have been replaced by supermarkets and shopping centers, selling everything from groceries to electronics to clothes. Services can also be found in downtown areas and in shopping centers. Hairdressers, lawyers, restaurants, and opticians all offer their expertise from their stores and offices.

COMMODITIES ARE PROCESSED USING...

... MANUFACTURED

Something special

There are also markets that specialize in one kind of product. In coastal towns, for example, there is often a fish market. The goods at specialized markets aren't usually sold to the general public, but to people who will process the food in some way. For example, a farmer may sell his crop of corn to a miller who grinds it to make flour. It's not only agricultural produce that's sold in these specialized markets. Just as fish markets and corn exchanges emerged from the general marketplace, so did markets to exchange goods like iron, coal, and diamonds—often in industrial cities and ports.

Buying and selling

Together, all the goods that are sold in these specialized markets are known as commodities, and are sold in specific commodity markets. The goods in these markets, which range from coffee and tea to metals and plastics, are usually sold in large quantities, and aren't physically taken to the market—instead, this is simply a place where traders meet to agree on a price and make a deal. Often, the traders aren't buying and selling for themselves, but selling on behalf of producers such as farmers, or buying on behalf of industries that process the goods in some way, such as food-

STOCK MARKETS

The stock market is where people buy shares, or stock, in companies. There are stock exchange buildings in cities like New York, London, and Tokyo. There is also a virtual market for electronic transactions, the NASDAQ (National Association of Securities Dealers Automated Quotations).

processing companies. In all these different kinds of market, whether it's a simple market stall, a department store, or a commodity market, the principle of buying and selling is the same. They provide a means of distributing resources, and a way of balancing supply—what the sellers have to offer—with demand—what the buyers are looking for.

See also: 36–37

ALL COMMODITIES, AS VALUES, ARE REALIZED HUMAN LABOR.
KARL MARX

GOODS...

... THAT NEED SERVICING.

Keeping up with CURRENCY

The first banknotes, called *jiaozi*, appeared in China between CE 970–1279.

BEFORE THE INVENTION OF MONEY, PEOPLE USED TO BARTER OR EXCHANGE GOODS AND SERVICES WITH ONE ANOTHER. THIS DEPENDED ON EACH PERSON IN THE TRANSACTION HAVING SOMETHING THE OTHER WANTED. TO GET AROUND THIS, THEY NEEDED TO FIND SOMETHING THAT WOULD BE ACCEPTED BY EVERYBODY AS HAVING WORTH, A CURRENCY, THAT THEY COULD USE TO BUY AND SELL THINGS.

What's it worth?

Forms of currency were developed in the ancient world to replace the awkward system of bartering, which was dependent on the person you wished to trade with needing something that you had to offer in return. But these currencies were not money as we know it today. Instead, they used commodities that were necessary or useful, such as sacks of corn or barley, as a medium of exchange. This "commodity money" could be used to buy all kinds of different goods, which were priced in terms of a certain weight of grain. It wasn't only food that was considered to have worth, though. Many societies prized precious stones and metals, or even seashells, and these too

> **GOLD STILL REPRESENTS THE ULTIMATE FORM OF PAYMENT IN THE WORLD.**
> ALAN GREENSPAN, FORMER CHAIR OF THE US FEDERAL RESERVE

were used as currency. One advantage of using these was that, in addition to being recognized as valuable, they don't deteriorate over time and are more convenient as a currency than large quantities of grain. In the ancient civilizations of the Mediterranean and Middle East, gold and silver became the primary medium of exchange, and goods changed hands for a set weight of these precious metals.

THE GOLD STANDARD

The gold standard was used by countries to stabilize their currencies by fixing their value to a scarce, valued resource: gold. A currency, such as the dollar, was valued as the same as a certain weight of gold. The government, which held a reserve of gold, issued bills and coins that could then be exchanged for gold on demand.

Coins and banknotes

For convenience, people began to produce pieces of these metals in specific weights, often in the form of small disks that were easy to carry. To make life easier, the weight of the metal was stamped on each piece, making them the first recognizable coins. As the use of these coins spread, they were stamped with a mark of authority, such as the head of the country's ruler, to show that they were of a standard weight and quality. Money in the form of coins was adopted globally, and continues today.

The idea of commodity money, pricing goods by their equivalent value of gold or silver, for example,

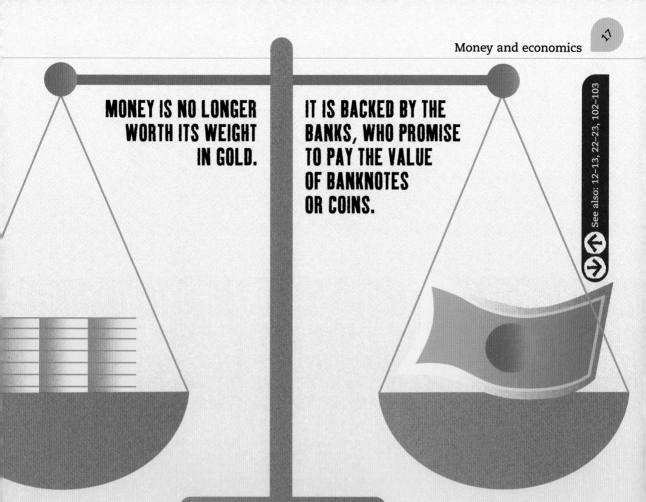

MONEY IS NO LONGER WORTH ITS WEIGHT IN GOLD.

IT IS BACKED BY THE BANKS, WHO PROMISE TO PAY THE VALUE OF BANKNOTES OR COINS.

See also: 12–13, 22–23, 102–103

evolved. If someone deposited a sum of money in the form of coins in a bank, the bank issued a receipt on a piece of paper. This could be used if the person later wanted to withdraw the money. Over time, these receipts came to be accepted as money in the same way as the coins. This "paper money" in the form of banknotes—literally notes from the bank—had no actual worth, except as a promise to pay an amount of gold or silver money.

Legal tender
Although coins continued as currency, they also changed. Once it became clear that money didn't need any real worth, countries began to make coins of nonprecious metals. These, like banknotes, are worth little, but represent

an amount of money, and can be used in exchange for something valuable. The system of using something that is nearly worthless as a means of payment is known as "*fiat* money" (from the Latin *fiat*, meaning "let it be done"), and they are referred to as "legal tender." The value of these coins and notes is declared by the banks or governments that issue them, and is fixed by law in most countries.

⬆ **Paper gold**
A banknote has almost no value in itself but represents a promise by a bank that the declared amount, originally of gold, will be paid to the bearer of the note.

THE PROCESS BY WHICH BANKS CREATE MONEY IS SO SIMPLE THAT THE MIND IS REPELLED.
JOHN KENNETH GALBRAITH

Fair EXCHANGE

MONEY IS USED IN EVERY PART OF THE WORLD TO BUY AND SELL, TO PAY PEOPLE FOR THEIR WORK, AND TO PUT A PRICE ON THINGS. BUT MONEY IS NOT THE SAME EVERYWHERE. DIFFERENT COUNTRIES AND REGIONS HAVE DIFFERENT UNITS OF MONEY, OR CURRENCIES, SUCH AS THE US DOLLAR, THE BRITISH POUND, AND THE JAPANESE YEN.

There are 180 currencies recognized by the United Nations as legal tender.

The language of money

Normally, the government of a country is in charge of producing the money that makes up its currency. It oversees the making of coins and banknotes, in a factory called a mint, which are then issued through banks. Because it's authorized by the government as "legal tender" (see p. 16), people can trust this money when it's used to pay for things. Each country has its own government that decides which unit of currency to use. So, just as different languages have evolved in different countries, so have different currencies, and people can use their money in exchange for goods and services within their own country. As with languages, there can be issues using currencies in other countries. If you go abroad, you need to have the money used in that country to buy things. For example, visitors to Paris from New York need to exchange US dollars for euros.

The price of money

Many products that we use aren't produced in our own country, but come from abroad and have to be imported. Companies also sell their products to customers around the world. This international trade often involves transactions between people using different currencies. To do this, there has to be a way of exchanging money from one currency to another. People traveling abroad can get foreign currency at a bank or a *bureau de change*, a business that specializes in exchanging money. They offer money at a particular exchange rate—the amount of foreign currency that they will give in exchange for one US dollar, for example. The exchange rate is also used when countries trade with one another. A US company can offer its goods for sale giving the price in US dollars, and customers can use the exchange rate to see how much that is in their own currency, and then change their money into dollars to buy them.

Strong and weak

When people exchange their money for another currency, they are effectively buying foreign money. Although it may seem strange to think of buying and selling money, this is exactly what the banks and *bureaux de change* do, and the exchange rate is the price of that money.

THE EURO

After World War II, many European countries came together to promote peace and to be trading partners. The idea of instituting a single currency in the European Union to replace the different currencies of the member countries took hold. In 1999, the euro (€) was created for electronic transactions, and in 2002 coins and banknotes were issued in the countries of the "Eurozone."

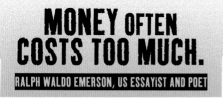

MONEY OFTEN COSTS TOO MUCH.
RALPH WALDO EMERSON, US ESSAYIST AND POET

In this sense, currencies are just like any other commodity that can be bought and sold. In fact, there are specialized markets that deal in foreign exchange, or "forex," trading. It's in these markets that the prices of the various currencies, and so the exchange rates, are set, according to how much demand there is for them. Because of this, the rates of exchange can vary from day to day, affecting the prices of

goods that are traded internationally. However, the exchange rate decided by the market, and so the amount of a foreign currency you get for your money, may not be an accurate guide to what you can buy with it in the other country. The currencies of smaller and poorer countries aren't as much in demand as major currencies like the dollar, yen, or euro, so their value is lower. When a visitor from a rich country travels to these countries, he can buy more with his strong currency than he would be able to at home. There is therefore often a big difference between the "nominal exchange rate" offered by the banks, and the real rate of exchange.

đ **$** **CURRENCIES ARE A BIT LIKE LANGUAGES...** **¥**

₽

$ **Rs**

TO BUY THINGS IN A COUNTRY YOU MUST HAVE THE CURRENCY OF THAT COUNTRY. THIS MEANS EXCHANGING YOUR USUAL CURRENCY FOR ANOTHER. BY DOING SO YOU ARE IN EFFECT BUYING MONEY.

Where did the

TODAY WE ARE USING CASH, THE COINS AND BILLS, OR BANKNOTES, WE HAVE IN OUR WALLETS, LESS AND LESS. INSTEAD, WE PAY FOR THINGS USING A CARD OR EVEN OUR SMARTPHONES. IN THESE TRANSACTIONS, WE CANNOT SEE OR TOUCH THE MONEY WE'RE SPENDING; IT DOESN'T EXIST IN A PHYSICAL FORM. SO, WHERE HAS ALL THE MONEY GONE?

A matter of trust

Physical money—coins and banknotes—isn't actually worth very much in itself. It is just bits of paper and cheap metal, but it has a value because we can exchange it for the things we want to buy (see pp. 16–17). When we purchase things with money, the people who take our money accept it because they know they can exchange it for other things, too. This trade is a matter of trust. We only accept this paper and metal money as payment because we believe it can be used to pay for other things. What we are doing when we pay for something with this kind of money is making a promise that the other person can buy things with it, too. In fact, the first banknotes were exactly that—signed notes promising that a bank would exchange them for something with real value, such as gold. The idea of a "promissory note" also developed into the system of checks. Rather than keeping all your money as cash, you can put it into a bank, in a bank account, and either withdraw it in small amounts or write a check when you need to pay for something. A check is simply a promise

that the bank will pay the other person with money from your account. In practice, though, what happens is that no physical money changes hands. The amount of money written on the check is deducted from your bank account and credited to the account of the person you are paying. The bank doesn't actually move any gold or silver, or even any cash, from one place to another, but simply changes the numbers in its records, either on paper or, more likely today, in computer memory.

Going electronic

With advances in technology, even the piece of paper a check is written on has become unnecessary. Debit and credit cards with computer chips have almost completely replaced those paper transactions. When a payment is made, the amount is automatically deducted from one account and credited to another. Instead of a signature,

Cashless ➔
While we may still use cash for buying small everyday items, we are increasingly making purchases online or even through our phones.

MONEY go?

we now often use a PIN (personal identification number) or password. We can also use these to make purchases online and electronically transfer money from one account to another. In addition to payments for goods that we buy, more and more of us are having our paychecks paid directly into our bank accounts by electronic transfer. Our financial transactions are increasingly becoming electronic and, except for small purchases, we are tending to use far less cash. We can access our accounts and make some purchases directly from our smartphones (see box below). Even the comparatively small amounts of cash that we do use, we often get from our banks electronically, using our debit cards at an ATM (automated teller machine).

97% of all money that "exists" today, only exists in virtual form.

ALL **MONEY** IS A MATTER OF **BELIEF.**
ADAM SMITH

Keeping it real

There is still a large amount of cash in circulation. This is partly because it is still useful for everyday transactions involving only small amounts. There are also still some people who trust what they consider "real" money—cash—more than the invisible and intangible money of electronic transactions. Nevertheless, the vast majority of money is now "virtual" money, reminding us that money is, after all, only worth what we believe it to be worth.

MOST MODERN MONEY DOESN'T EXIST IN PHYSICAL FORM

MONEY ONLINE

Money, or at least coins and banknotes, is still useful today for making small payments, such as buying a coffee. But with smartcards, and apps for our smartphones, even these transactions are becoming increasingly cashless. Soon, perhaps face, fingerprint, and voice recognition machines will make it possible to touch a button or give a command to pay for things.

CRYPTOCURRENCIES

ADVANCES IN COMPUTER TECHNOLOGY HAVE CHANGED THE WAY WE DO BUSINESS. WE CAN BUY THINGS ONLINE FROM SELLERS ANYWHERE IN THE WORLD, AND MONEY GOES IN AND OUT OF OUR BANK ACCOUNTS WITHOUT OUR ACTUALLY SEEING OR TOUCHING IT. THERE ARE EVEN CURRENCIES THAT EXIST ONLY IN DIGITAL FORM.

DIGITAL CURRENCY

With the increase of online transactions, electronic transfers of money became more and more commonplace. This idea of "electronic money" inspired the invention of a number of new purely electronic currencies in the 1990s as an internet-based medium of exchange. Some of these "virtual currencies" are only accepted within virtual communities, but there are also digital currencies that are accepted in the real world, such as the bitcoin.

DECENTRALIZED CURRENCIES

All money is becoming increasingly "electronic," as more of it exists only in the memory of banks' computers. But truly digital currencies, which are not managed by a central bank, have also evolved. They use peer-to-peer payment systems, in which users make transactions directly. These decentralized currencies are also independent of governments, relying on the trust of the users rather than a central authority.

Bitcoin became the first decentralized cryptocurrency in 2009.

"The relative success of the **bitcoin** proves that **money** first and foremost **depends on trust**."

AARON GRUNBERG, DUTCH NEWSPAPER COLUMNIST

CRYPTOGRAPHY

Rather than being backed by reserves of gold or government bonds, some digital currency has a value based simply on the confidence of its users. Money in the system is created by a network of users, using cryptography, a form of information security with complex codes. The first of these cryptocurrencies, as they are known, was the bitcoin, and it was followed by a number of others, which are often called altcoins.

THE DOWNSIDE

Just like conventional money, electronic money has a downside. Banks are constantly updating their computer security, but criminals are often only one step behind. The new digital currencies, even the most sophisticated cryptocurrencies, are not immune to cybercrime. New systems and technology must constantly evolve to make our transactions safer and more convenient.

CLASSICAL SCHOOL

MARXIST SCHOOL

NEOCLASSICAL SCHOOL

AUSTRIAN SCHOOL

ADAM SMITH
(1723–90)
THE WEALTH OF
NATIONS
PUBLISHED 1776

KARL MARX (1818–83)
THE COMMUNIST
MANIFESTO
PUBLISHED 1848;
DAS KAPITAL PUBLISHED
1867, 1885, 1894

ALFRED MARSHALL
(1842–1924)
PRINCIPLES OF
ECONOMICS
PUBLISHED 1890

FRIEDRICH HAYEK
(1899–1992)
THE ROAD TO SERFDOM
PUBLISHED 1944

Making SENSE of

PEOPLE HAVE BEEN THINKING ABOUT THE WAYS THAT WE MANAGE OUR RESOURCES, AND DISTRIBUTE GOODS AND SERVICES, SINCE THE FIRST CIVILIZATIONS WERE ESTABLISHED. OVER THE CENTURIES, THERE HAVE BEEN MANY DIFFERENT EXPLANATIONS OF HOW OUR ECONOMIES WORK, AND THE BEST WAYS TO MANAGE THEM.

95% OF ECONOMICS IS COMMON SENSE ... MADE COMPLICATED.
HA-JOON CHANG

See also: 12–13, 14–15

Enlightened thinking

The subject of economics as we know it didn't emerge until the late 18th century. During the Enlightenment, when thinkers and scientists were challenging conventional ideas, Adam Smith (see p. 32), a Scotsman, developed a new way of thinking about economics. Smith, along with other thinkers, looked at the way goods are produced and traded. Previously people thought trade was largely a matter of gaining something at the expense of others, but he proposed that both participants in a transaction could benefit. These ideas laid the foundations of modern economics, and together they are called the Classical school.

Power to the people

It's no coincidence that these new ideas emerged in Britain at this time. The country was changing from a mainly agricultural economy to one of the first industrial nations, and society was changing. The Industrial Revolution, as this became known, brought with it increased prosperity for the owners of the factories and mills, but also poverty for workers in the new industries. Karl Marx (see p. 48) thought that this was unjust, and a failure of the market economy to distribute wealth fairly. He recommended that the factories and other means of production should be taken from their owners, the capitalists, and handed over to the control of the workers so that they could benefit directly from their work. While Marx's ideas were later adopted by a number of communist states, many economists rejected them, believing in the power of the market to distribute resources. Toward

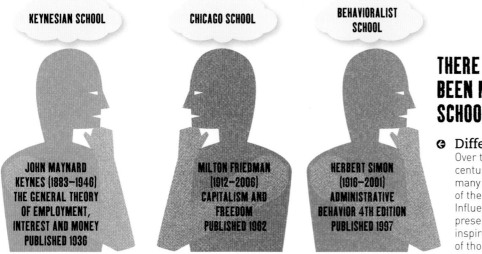

KEYNESIAN SCHOOL

CHICAGO SCHOOL

BEHAVIORALIST SCHOOL

JOHN MAYNARD KEYNES (1883–1946) THE GENERAL THEORY OF EMPLOYMENT, INTEREST AND MONEY PUBLISHED 1936

MILTON FRIEDMAN (1912–2006) CAPITALISM AND FREEDOM PUBLISHED 1962

HERBERT SIMON (1916–2001) ADMINISTRATIVE BEHAVIOR 4TH EDITION PUBLISHED 1997

THERE HAVE ALWAYS BEEN MANY ECONOMIC SCHOOLS OF THOUGHT

↻ Differences of opinion
Over the last two and a half centuries, there have been many different interpretations of the subject of economics. Influential economists have presented new ideas and inspired distinctive schools of thought.

economics

See also: 30–31, 66–67

the end of the 19th century, Alfred Marshall (1842-1924) and Léon Walras (1834-1910) among others, established Neoclassical economics, describing and explaining Classical theories using scientific and mathematical principles.

Free market
The so-called Austrian school of economists reacted more strongly to Marx's ideas. In particular, Friedrich Hayek pointed out the failures of communist governments to manage prosperous economies. The Austrian school argued that governments had too much control and did not leave individual people and businesses to operate freely. Their suggestion of markets totally free of regulation or intervention, a *laissez-faire* economy, was also taken up by economists such as Milton Friedman of the Chicago school.

Preventing failure
During the 1930s, the Great Depression (see pp. 74-75) showed that the market could fail, too. One of the most influential of 20th-century economists, John Maynard Keynes (see p. 111) put forward his theories

"Economics" comes from the Greek meaning "household management."

of how a certain amount of government intervention and control could help to prevent such failures.

Learning from the past
Each of these schools of economic thought was a product of its time but many of the principles can still be applied today. Economists can look back on which of these theories has proved to work best in the real world, and adapt and improve upon them.

IS ECONOMICS A SCIENCE?
Many economists have considered their subject as a kind of science. But economics is not a "hard science" like physics. Money is not a natural phenomenon, but a human invention, shaped by our behavior and influenced by political ideas. Economics is not an exact science—it can be hard to prove a theory right or wrong.

CLONE ATTACK

One of the drawbacks of coins and banknotes is that they can be easily forged. Throughout history, forgers have made "gold" coins out of cheaper metals and printed fake bills and banknotes. But the cost of forgery is high, and often not worth it—cloning bankcards can bring much greater rewards.

NEW ECONOMIC IDEAS

There have been many different theories in economics, some of them directly contradicting others. This is because the economy itself is constantly changing, with advances in technology and ways of doing business, and economists develop new theories to fit the changing world.

Money and economics
IN PRACTICE

PREDICTING THE FUTURE

Economists describe and explain how the economy works. But economics is not a "hard science" in which a theory can be proved right or wrong. Some suggest how the economy should be managed and what will happen if we act a certain way. But it's unpredictable and their forecasts can be disastrously wrong.

CASH IN HAND

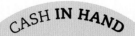

Even though we can pay for things electronically, many people prefer to use cash. Some even feel they can trust cash more, because they can see and hold it. The downside is that it can be lost or stolen and, unlike cards and electronic currency, it isn't safeguarded.

People in rich countries often take a constant supply of essential resources for granted. In poorer countries, a natural resource like water may be in short supply. And even when there is enough of a resource, it may not be evenly distributed. Some resources, such as oil, will run out one day. It's an economist's job to suggest ways to manage these resources.

FINITE RESOURCES

In the 20th century, economics became divided into two fields: microeconomics and macroeconomics. Some economists focused on the behavior of individual people and companies, or microeconomics. Others concentrated on macro-economics—the economics of a country or the world as a whole.

MACRO- AND MICROECONOMICS

The way in which money and markets work affects us in everyday life—every time we use our bank accounts or buy something in a store. Advances in technology are changing the way we use money, but the same principles apply whether we carry currency or handle our business online.

The idea of a single world currency has been around for a long time. But while each country has its own government, this seems impossible. The nearest we have is the US dollar, which is accepted in some countries alongside the local currency, or the new virtual currencies such as the bitcoin.

ONE MONEY

DAYLIGHT ROBBERY

Today, many banks don't have much cash in them, so the smartest bank robbers don't run into a bank with a sack and a shotgun. Instead, they work from a computer, hacking into the bank's accounts and moving the money electronically, this makes cybersecurity the priority for banks these days.

What's it WORTH?

The economic PROBLEM

Who gets WHAT?

GOODS and services

SUPPLY and DEMAND

Why are some things more VALUABLE?

The goods that we need are supplied by businesses, such as the agricultural and manufacturing industries, and sold to us through markets. The price we pay for them—how much we value them—depends on how scarce or plentiful the resources are, how much demand there is for these goods, and whether this demand is being met by the supply.

A hive of INDUSTRY

Healthy COMPETITION?

Who's in CHARGE?

How businesses OPERATE

Running an EFFICIENT business

Going to WORK

BIG spenders

The economic PROBLEM

The population of the world is predicted to be 9.6 billion by the year 2050.

ECONOMICS IS NOT ALL ABOUT MONEY. WHILE MONEY IS AN IMPORTANT PART OF THE SUBJECT, ECONOMICS IS CONCERNED WITH THE WAY WE MANAGE OUR RESOURCES, HOW WE USE WHAT IS AVAILABLE TO US TO SATISFY EVERYBODY'S NEEDS AND WANTS. THIS IS SOMETIMES REFERRED TO SIMPLY AS "THE ECONOMIC PROBLEM."

What we want and need

Our needs and wants change constantly and seem to be unlimited, but the things we need to meet these demands are limited. Economists use the word "scarcity" to describe this situation: a thing is said to be scarce when there is less of it than is required. If whatever we wanted was available in unlimited quantities, there would be no problem satisfying our unlimited needs. Practically, however, resources are scarce, and fall short of requirements as much in rich countries as in poor. There are many different kinds of resources that economists have identified as necessary. The most obvious ones are natural resources, such as water, that we obtain directly from the environment. They also include plants that grow

THE EARTH PROVIDES ENOUGH TO **SATISFY** EVERY MAN'S **NEED** BUT NOT FOR EVERY MAN'S **GREED.**

MAHATMA GANDHI

DISASTER!

Resources are not spread evenly around the world and are scarcer in some regions than in others. Food and water, for example, are abundant in some places, but in others people have barely enough to stay alive. Unless they have other resources, such as oil, their economies are precarious and vulnerable to disasters like drought, crop failure, or disease.

MATCHING LIMITED RESOURCES TO UNLIMITED NEEDS AND WANTS...

SOLVING THE ECONOMIC PROBLEM MEANS FINDING ANSWERS TO QUESTIONS SUCH AS WHAT TO PRODUCE, HOW BEST TO PRODUCE IT, AND WHO TO PRODUCE IT FOR.

See also: 32–33, 38–39

naturally, or animals that live in the wild, which we can use for food. There are also ways we can use the land, by farming to produce crops or by mining to extract resources such as coal.

Sometimes called "land resources"—but which include resources we get from the sea—these provide us with raw materials to produce goods we need. But the amount of land in the world is finite and can't provide unlimited resources. While we can continue growing food, or using renewable energy sources like sun or wind power, other resources will eventually run out.

Making things

Some resources do not occur naturally, but are produced from raw materials. These man-made resources, known as capital goods, include machinery, buildings like factories, and transportation such as railroads, which are used in the production and distribution of goods. To make these things, we need another kind of resource: labor. Human resources, in the form of working people, are a vital part of producing goods and services. In addition to physical labor, human resources include skills, knowledge, and information.

Managing resources

Each society has access to some or all of these resources. But it may also have a growing population, with needs and wants that are changing rapidly.

Solving the problem of matching demand with limited resources involves making choices and decisions, and finding an answer to three basic questions. First, what goods and services should it produce? Many resources could be used to produce several different things. For example, land could be used to grow essential food crops, or grapes for wine, and a large building could be either a hospital or a luxury hotel. Second, how best can it produce goods and services? Some countries have few natural resources, but their large populations provide a strong labor resource. If they concentrate on the goods and services they can produce most efficiently, they can earn money to import the things they need. Third, who are the goods and services produced for? It isn't possible to produce everything that everyone needs or wants, so each society has to find a way of deciding who will benefit from its resources, and how the goods and services are distributed among its members.

Who gets WHAT?

OF COURSE, WE SHOULD PRODUCE THINGS THAT PEOPLE NEED AND WANT, BUT HOW DO WE DECIDE ON THE ALLOCATION OF OUR RESOURCES? AND HOW DO WE MAKE SURE THE GOODS AND SERVICES WE PRODUCE ARE DISTRIBUTED TO THE PEOPLE WHO NEED AND WANT THEM?

> PERHAPS A DAY MIGHT COME WHEN THERE WOULD BE ENOUGH TO GO ROUND, AND WHEN PROSPERITY COULD ENTER INTO THE ENJOYMENT OF OUR LABORS.
>
> JOHN MAYNARD KEYNES

Who decides?

We do not have an infinite supply of resources such as land and labor. The problem is that they can be used to produce different things so we have to decide how best to use them to meet our needs and wants. In addition to this allocation of resources, there is the question of who should get the things that are produced, how the goods and services should be distributed. Finding a solution to the "economic problem" of matching resources with needs and wants is important to the well-being of every society. Because governments have the responsibility of ensuring the welfare of their people, perhaps they should make the decisions about how resources are allocated?

In 2007, a portrait of Adam Smith was featured on the £20 banknote issued by the Bank of England.

Smith's solution

An 18th-century Scottish economist, Adam Smith (see pp. 16–17), argued that while this decision should be made for the good of society as a whole, it could best be made by individuals acting in their own interests. Although the idea seems illogical, Smith explained that it is the way that goods and services are bought and sold that determines how resources are allocated. In a market, whenever things are bought and sold, the individual traders and customers do not think about what is best for society as a whole, but just about what is good for themselves. Customers go out to buy what they need or want to satisfy their self-interest. Suppliers sell their goods, not out of public-spiritedness, but because they want to make money. They can only sell if there are customers who want their goods, so they produce goods that there is a market for and they stop producing goods for which there is no demand. It is the market, made up of individual transactions, that matches goods with the customers' wants and needs. Smith described the action of the market as being like an invisible hand that guides us to the most efficient allocation of resources, and a fair distribution of goods and services. Each individual, either as a customer or supplier, makes perfectly rational decisions about what to buy or sell, in their own self-interest, but collectively these act for the good of society as a whole. In a perfect market, supply and

ADAM SMITH (1723–90)

Born in Scotland, Adam Smith is widely regarded as the father of modern economics. He was a professor of philosophy at Glasgow University and one of a group of thinkers that included the philosopher David Hume. In the 1760s, Smith traveled to France and began work on *An Inquiry into the Nature and Causes of the Wealth of Nations*, which he finished in 1776.

See also: 30-31

BUSINESSES ONLY PRODUCE PRODUCTS FOR WHICH THERE IS A DEMAND.

demand will eventually balance one another, and ensure the best possible distribution of goods. What's more, in a perfect market, the buyer and seller both do well out of the deal. Customers get the goods and services they want, and suppliers make a profit from selling their goods.

It's not fair!

Not all economists agreed with Smith. Many have pointed out situations where the market fails to work efficiently, benefitting only a few people (see pp. 74–75). To prevent this, governments have to regulate the markets in some ways. Others, notably Karl Marx, argued that the market is inherently unfair and prone to ups and downs, with fluctuations of supply and demand, and that governments, not markets should decide on the allocation of resources.

Meeting demand ➌

A producer will offer goods for sale where people need or want them. If there are no customers for the goods the producer will stop making them.

ETHICAL TRADE

MANY PEOPLE THINK TRADE SHOULD BE ETHICAL AS WELL AS FREE. ETHICAL TRADE MEANS THAT BUSINESSES DON'T SIMPLY SELL GOODS FOR THE BEST PRICE. THEY MUST ALSO CONSIDER THE EFFECT OF THEIR BUSINESS ON, FOR INSTANCE, THE WORKING CONDITIONS OF THE PEOPLE THEY EMPLOY OR THE IMPACT ON THE ENVIRONMENT.

TAKE A STAND

Consumers in the developed world can push businesses to do the right thing through boycotts. In 2013, the Rana Plaza clothing factory in Bangladesh collapsed, killing over 1,100 people. The clothing chains Primark and Benetton, supplied by the factory, faced protests. Since then, there's been pressure for clothing retailers to ensure safety in the factories where their garments are made, and to give details of where their goods come from.

Over a fifth of coffee is now Fair trade, and nearly two-thirds of UK consumers buy Fair-trade bananas.

BUYING ETHICALLY

Ethical consumerism means that buyers pressure businesses to behave well through what they choose to buy. Businesses then respond by creating products that are "sustainably sourced" or "free range." When choosing a bank, people may avoid one that invests in the arms trade or polluting industries. Ethical banks consider environmental and social impacts when investing and making loans.

⬆ A fine balance

To trade ethically means balancing the effects of the business on the environment and on the workers involved with the need to generate a profit.

> "With **Fair Trade**, farmers get a **fair price** for their harvest with a guaranteed minimum, so they can **invest** in their crops."
>
> **NELL NEWMAN, US ENVIRONMENTALIST**

FAIR TRADE

The Fair trade movement began in the 1990s to prevent coffee and banana growers in poor countries from losing out because of low market prices. Fair-trade organizations guarantee suppliers a fair price. In return, suppliers ensure workers are properly paid and employed. Consumers support this by buying Fair-trade certified goods. This works when prices are low, but when prices rise suppliers lose out.

EXPLOITED WORKERS

To stay competitive, businesses cut costs, and may turn a blind eye to the conditions of workers making goods for them. In recent years, consumers in the developed world have become aware that many of the goods they purchase so cheaply in stores, such as clothing and electrical goods, are produced in less developed countries—in factories where safety is neglected, in sweatshops, and by child or even slave labor. This has forced businesses to change their production procedures and be more transparent about them.

GOODS and

In the US an estimated 80% of the workforce is in the service sector, contributing around 80% of GDP.

IN ECONOMICS, THINGS THAT ARE BOUGHT AND SOLD ARE CALLED GOODS. THESE INCLUDE COMMODITIES SUCH AS FOOD AND MANUFACTURED GOODS SUCH AS COMPUTERS. THERE ARE ALSO INTANGIBLE GOODS THAT CANNOT BE PHYSICALLY HELD OR SEEN— THESE ARE THINGS THAT PEOPLE DO IN RETURN FOR MONEY; THEY ARE ALSO CALLED SERVICES.

Objects of desire

Goods are the things that people need or want, that will be useful to them, or that they consider desirable. But more than that, they are things that they consider valuable enough to exchange money for, to purchase. Because there are people who want to buy these goods, there will be other people who make their living from supplying them. The supply side of the market, as opposed to the demand side—the customers—is made up of many different kinds of business, all producing different kinds of goods. For example, there are farmers who provide agricultural goods such as crops and livestock produced from working the land. There are also businesses that use the land to provide other necessary goods. Mining companies, for example, extract the raw materials for making metals, and other minerals from the ground. Other companies mine for coal, or drill for oil and gas that can be used to provide our energy.

> A LITTLE OVER 5% OF THE WORLD'S POPULATION PRODUCES ALMOST 29% OF THE WORLD'S GOODS.
>
> STEPHEN COVEY, "THE SEVEN HABITS OF HIGHLY EFFECTIVE PEOPLE"

BUSINESSES PROVIDE GOODS AND SERVICES

GOODS

Making and doing ❯

People are employed in different sectors of the economy, providing raw materials, producing manufactured goods, or offering services.

services

Manufactured goods

Aside from food, the majority of goods that we buy are manufactured goods. That is, they have been made from raw materials, in a factory, or by a craftsperson. Manufacturing industries produce a huge range of capital goods (see box, opposite) and consumer goods, from necessities such as clothes, through household items such as furniture, to appliances such as washing machines, ovens, and cars. Almost all the things that we buy are goods that have been manufactured in some way, whether it's by a large factory that mass-produces particular goods, or a small workshop making handcrafted, luxury items. In addition to the manufactured goods that we have in our homes, we need the houses themselves to live in. Buildings are also a kind of good, and are produced by the construction industries. In addition to providing housing, the construction industry also produces buildings for commercial use, such as factories, offices, hotels, railroad stations, and stores.

Service sector

While industries such as agriculture and mining provide raw materials, and manufacturing and construction industries produce tangible goods, there is a third sector of industry that does not make a tangible product—something that a buyer can physically own and keep. Instead, these businesses offer a service. Some services are closely connected with physical goods, for example, transportation companies that collect goods from a farmer or a factory and then deliver them to customers. There are also many different types of retail businesses, which buy goods from manufacturers and sell them to the general public through their stores. The service sector also includes businesses that offer things as straightforward as a haircut or a taxi ride, or essential services such as health care or education, or repair businesses like auto mechanics and building maintenance firms. There are services that many of us use every day, including public transportation and telecommunications, or banking and insurance services. Then there are others, such as hotels and movie theaters, that we use less often and consider luxuries to be indulged in during our leisure time.

Working to serve

Today, more and more people work in the service sector, especially in the richer countries. This is partly because mechanization of the older agricultural and manufacturing industries has made them more efficient, so they use fewer workers to produce more goods. But it is also because our needs have changed now that we have more money and more leisure time.

CAPITAL GOODS

The goods we notice most are consumer goods, the things sold in stores. But there are also things such as machinery, buildings, and transportation, known as capital goods, that are produced for industries and used in the making of consumer goods and in services.

SERVICES

SUPPLY and DEMAND

CONSUMERS AND PRODUCERS COME TOGETHER IN THE MARKET TO BUY AND SELL GOODS. THEIR TRANSACTIONS MATCH DEMAND – THE QUANTITY OF GOODS THE BUYER WANTS – WITH SUPPLY – THE QUANTITY THE SELLER OFFERS. BUT SUPPLY AND DEMAND ARE ALSO AFFECTED BY THE PRICE OF THE GOODS.

> THE MORE OF A THING **OFFERED** THE **LOWER** IS THE PRICE AT WHICH IT WILL FIND PURCHASERS.
> **ALFRED MARSHALL**

Strike a deal

In a traditional street market the prices of goods are not rigidly fixed. Many traders expect their customers to haggle, to negotiate a price that they both agree on. Buyers think about how much they want or need the goods, and how much they are prepared to pay. The sellers weigh up how low they are prepared to drop the price to make a sale without losing money on the deal. The interaction between buyer and seller determines the price, the amount that changes hands. This interaction is affected by the quantity of the goods available: the supply, and the number of customers wanting them: the demand. For the sale to work, however, it has to be a competitive market in which there is more than one supplier

of goods, and more than one buyer. This gives the buyer the chance to shop around, compare prices, and use them to negotiate a good deal. Sellers compete to offer the lowest prices, but benefit when demand is high enough for buyers to seek out goods that are in scarce supply.

Time it right

The price of goods is closely related to their supply and demand. For example, farmers produce wheat that they can sell to mills to make flour. At harvest time, the wheat is plentiful, and the farmers have more wheat than the mills need. Supply is greater than demand and there is a surplus, so the suppliers drop their prices to try to sell more. During the winter, the demand for flour is the same, but farmers don't have as much wheat as the mills need. Now the mills are prepared to pay more for the wheat, and the price goes up. The same is true of all goods and services. If demand

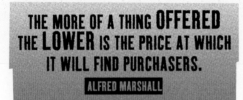

Price: what a buyer pays for goods.
Cost: what a seller has paid to get goods to the market.

See also: 30–31, 32–33

WHEN GOODS ARE SCARCE, BUYERS COMPETE AND PRICES ARE HIGHER

WHEN THERE IS A SURPLUS, PRICES DROP TO ATTRACT BUYERS

Price impact

It also works the other way around and prices affect supply and demand. If there is a surplus of goods, prices fall but lower prices make the goods more attractive to buyers, and so stimulate an increase in demand. Higher prices put buyers off, but stimulate an increase in supply.

The ups and down of supply and demand, and of prices, are continually working in a competitive market to compensate for shortages and surpluses. In a perfect market, this means that the levels of supply and demand are always balanced, or in equilibrium, and this is reflected in the price of the goods.

remains the same but supply increases, the supplier will have a surplus, and prices will fall. If demand is the same and supply decreases, this results in a shortage, and higher prices. For goods that are in constant supply, it is changes in demand that affect the price: if demand falls, it causes a surplus, and prices fall, but if demand increases, there is a shortage and prices go up.

CREATING DEMAND

Producers of goods don't always supply goods that there is a demand for. Suppliers, especially if they have a new product to sell, will try to create a demand for their goods. By advertising, they hope to persuade people to buy things they didn't know they needed or wanted—especially if they are offered at apparently bargain prices.

Why are some VALUABLE?

THE PRICE OF GOODS OFFERED FOR SALE IN A MARKET IS DETERMINED BY SUPPLY AND DEMAND. BUT THE VALUE OF SOMETHING, WHAT WE THINK IT IS REALLY WORTH, DEPENDS ON OTHER THINGS, TOO. AND THIS VALUE WILL AFFECT THE DECISIONS THAT WE MAKE.

Less means more

When goods are in plentiful supply, the price of them is lower than when they are in short supply. It is easy to take for granted things that are readily available everywhere, and not value them very highly. There are even some things, such as the air we breathe, that are known as "free goods." This means that these goods are freely available to us all the time. On the other hand, there are things that are much rarer, such as gold and diamonds, for which we will pay large sums of money. Because the supply of these rare commodities is far less than the demand for them, they are said to have a "scarcity value." So, the less of something there is the more it is worth and the more of something there is the less it is worth.

Paradox of value

For example, if you are walking along a shingle riverbank and see a diamond glittering among the stones, you will probably pick it up and take it home. This is because you consider it to be valuable. More valuable than the other stones, and certainly more valuable than the water in the river. But in some ways your idea of what is valuable seems illogical. Water is essential for us to live, yet we do not value it as highly as a diamond, which has almost no immediate practical use. The answer to this "paradox of value" is that the diamond has scarcity value, while the water does not. The water is freely available and in plentiful supply.

What's the use?

In addition to this, we also get different kinds of pleasure or satisfaction from the two different goods. The satisfaction you get from having and using a good is known as "utility," and this changes with the amount of the good that you consume. If you get thirsty on your riverside walk, the first drop of water you have will be the most

GIFFEN GOODS

Scottish economist Robert Giffen (1837–1910) pointed out that there are some goods that don't seem to follow the rule of supply and demand. He argued that demand for these "Giffen goods" rises as their price goes up. For example, people with little money buy more bread when the price goes up, because at a certain point they can no longer afford to buy other, more expensive foods.

things more

satisfying, and after that each sip is slightly less so. The first diamond you find is thrilling, but because it takes time and effort to find another, the next diamond you find will be not quite so exciting. The more there is of something, the greater the decrease in marginal utility—or the satisfaction you get from each use of it. In economics, it is said that the marginal utility of each extra drop of water is very low, but the marginal utility of each extra diamond is very high.

Opportunity and time

A different way of explaining how we value things is in terms of what they cost us. This is not the price that is put on them, but what we have to give up in order to get them. You may have to choose, for example, whether to buy a new bike, or whether to use that money to take driving lessons. If you decide to learn to drive, you give up the opportunity of being able to ride around on your new bike, but gain in the long term by learning a skill that lasts a lifetime. What you give up—the "opportunity cost"—determines the value of the thing that you decide to keep.

Some economists explain the value of goods and services in another way. They believe that the true value of these things is determined by how much labor has gone into producing them. So, the value of manufactured goods, cars or computers, for example, depends on the number of people who were involved in making them and the amount of work they put in. This is known as the labor theory of value and it was first explained by Adam Smith (see pp. 18–19) and other Classical economists. It is also an important idea in Marxian economics.

... WE WOULD VALUE WATER MORE THAN DIAMONDS.

⊙ The paradox of value
Some things that have very little practical use, such as diamonds, are valued more highly than essentials such as water.

The world's biggest cut diamond is the Golden Jubilee Diamond, weighing 545.67 carats (3.85 oz/ 109.13 g) and worth $4–12 million.

According to the labor theory, two different goods that involved the same amount of work and took the same time to produce, should cost the same amount of money. If the cost of buying a good is more than the buyer values the time it would take to make it, then the buyer could make the good themselves.

A hive of INDUSTRY

THE WORD "INDUSTRY" USED TO CONJURE UP IMAGES OF FACTORIES BUZZING WITH MACHINERY. THIS KIND OF HEAVY MANUFACTURING INDUSTRY EMERGED IN THE 18TH CENTURY, TRANSFORMING SOCIETY AND THE ECONOMY. TODAY, TECHNOLOGICAL ADVANCES ARE AGAIN CHANGING THE WAY WE PRODUCE GOODS AND SERVICES.

See also: 14–15, 36–37

Working for a wage

Before the invention of industrial machinery, most people worked on the land, which was owned by a few royal or noble families. Peasant farmers grew crops and raised animals to provide food, cloth, and fuel. Agriculture, and to a lesser extent the mining of metals and minerals, formed the basis for the economy, and in many poor countries this is still the case. Things changed dramatically with the advent of mechanization. Mills could produce goods such as flour and cloth in huge quantities, and factories appeared that could mass-produce all kinds of

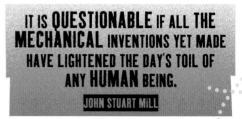

IT IS **QUESTIONABLE** IF ALL THE **MECHANICAL** INVENTIONS YET MADE HAVE LIGHTENED THE DAY'S TOIL OF ANY **HUMAN** BEING.

JOHN STUART MILL

manufactured goods. These mills and factories provided jobs, and many workers were attracted by the prospect of earning money rather than living off the land. As they moved from the country to where the work was, large industrial cities grew.

Growth and prosperity

There was a change too in the economic system. Rather than producing food for landowning masters, and keeping some for themselves, workers were paid a wage by the owners of the factories and mills. The owners were a new class of entrepreneurs, who owned the means of production—the buildings and machinery. These are sometimes known as capital goods, and so the owners were called capitalists, and the new system, capitalism. The new manufacturing industry, and the capitalist system it brought with it, spread

THE INDUSTRIAL REVOLUTION

In Britain in the 18th century, the pace of scientific discovery accelerated, and with it came inventions of machines such as steam engines that revolutionized the way goods were produced. Mechanized mills and factories, and the introduction of rail transportation, spawned new industries, and a dramatic change in the economic structure of society.

INDUSTRIALISATION ENCOURAGED CAPITALISM AND BROUGHT ABOUT ECONOMIC GROWTH

◉ Industry powers the economy

In the modern world, goods and services are produced by a range of different industries—from farming to online businesses—which are essential to economic growth and prosperity.

See also: 48–49, 56–57

industries appeared such as social media sites and online trading. In some rich countries, service industries are replacing traditional manufacturing industries and agriculture, so much so that some people believe we are moving into a "postindustrial" age. Goods may be imported rather than manufactured, but even societies whose economies are based largely on service industries need housing, food, and manufactured goods. Even the most technologically advanced countries continue to maintain traditional industries in the agricultural, manufacturing, and construction sectors for their own use, if not for export.

from Britain across Europe and America. Because mechanization meant that goods could be produced more cheaply and in greater quantities, it brought prosperity for the capitalist class. Since the Industrial Revolution, industries have kept improving their efficiency, which has made societies wealthier. It wasn't only manufacturing industries that benefitted. Agriculture, mining, and construction have also become increasingly mechanized, reducing costs and increasing production. Alongside these industries there was a need for services, such as construction and repairs, to keep them running smoothly, and financial services, such as banking and insurance. As societies grew richer, more people had money to spend on goods that had been seen as luxuries, or services that they used to do for themselves.

Agriculture still accounts for nearly 40% of the world's workforce.

What next?

In the late 20th century, electronic technology brought more change. Computers and information technology revolutionized many of the service industries, such as banking, and with the advent of the internet new

AGRICULTURAL AND SKILLED CRAFTS

MANUFACTURING INDUSTRIES

COMPUTERS AND INFORMATION TECHNOLOGY

PUBLIC COMPANIES

MANY BIG BUSINESSES ARE PUBLIC COMPANIES. THEY RAISE MONEY TO DEVELOP THEIR BUSINESS BY DIVIDING OWNERSHIP INTO EQUAL SHARES. THESE ARE SOLD TO THE PUBLIC WHO BECOME SHAREHOLDERS. PUBLIC COMPANIES ARE OWNED BY SHAREHOLDERS WHO ELECT A BOARD OF DIRECTORS TO RUN THE COMPANY FOR THEM.

LIMITED LIABILITY

If a public company fails and piles up huge debts, shareholders only ever have to pay the cost of their initial investment. The company alone is responsible for its debts. This is called "limited liability." Limited liability is the norm in most countries because too many investors would be put off by the risk of financial disaster if they were made liable for all of the company's debts.

"The **directors** of such companies cannot well be expected to **watch over other people's money** with the same anxious **vigilance** they **watch over their own."**

ADAM SMITH

SHAREHOLDERS

In return for their investment, all the shareholders receive an annual payment or "dividend," which varies with company profits. They also have a say in how the company is run. While directors run the company on a day-to-day basis, shareholders can use their influence to keep the company on a steady course. Public ownership is declining, as private companies, unhindered by shareholders, suit today's rapidly changing markets.

⊕ Slice of the cake

To raise money, businesses will sell off a part of their company. Those who buy the slices become shareholders who are able to influence how the company is run.

GOING BUST

When a company can't pay its debts, a court may declare it bankrupt. This isn't a punishment but a legal status in which the court is empowered to decide how to sort out the financial mess, and see what money can be retrieved to pay creditors. If bankrupt companies are punished harshly, investors may be put off from investing in future. But if debtors are let off too easily, creditors may be deterred from doing business.

Between 1997 and 2012, the number of public companies traded on the US stock exchange almost halved.

RAISING CAPITAL

Businesses go "public" in order to dramatically widen the sources of capital that can help it grow. Shareholders put money in either by buying stocks (shares in a company's assets or "equity") or by buying bonds (direct loans of money to the company). Both stocks and bonds can be bought and sold on, entirely independently, on stock and bond markets. So, the company itself becomes a commodity that can be traded.

Healthy
COMPETITION?

COMPETITION BETWEEN TRADERS IS AT THE HEART OF A FREE MARKET. COMPETITIVE MARKETS BENEFIT THE CONSUMER, AS THEY PUSH SELLERS TO KEEP THEIR PRICES DOWN TO SELL THEIR GOODS. IN TURN, THIS ENCOURAGES PRODUCERS TO WORK MORE EFFICIENTLY, REDUCING THEIR COSTS AND INCREASING PRODUCTIVITY, AND FINDING NEW WAYS TO MAKE NEW AND BETTER PRODUCTS.

A market for a product with many sellers and only one buyer is called a monopsony.

MONOPOLIES

When there is only one seller of a particular product, this is called a monopoly. Because a seller who holds a monopoly does not have to compete with others on price, the consumer generally has to pay more for the goods. Lack of competition also means that monopolies are less likely to worry about making their businesses more efficient.

Free market

It is not only the consumer who benefits from competitive markets. In the long run, producers are also rewarded by more sales and more productive industries. Efficient industries are good for society as a whole, making it more prosperous and better able to compete in the global market. The idea of a free market is simple: allow buyers and sellers to interact freely and they'll reach a deal that benefits everyone.

Fit for the market ➋
In a free-market economy, companies compete with one another for business, which encourages them to become more efficient and offer the best deal to their customers.

All good in theory, but in practice, there have to be some rules to stop people from taking advantage of the market. Most countries have laws regulating trade—to protect consumers from unscrupulous traders and workers from exploitative producers.

How free is free?

Economists have differing opinions as to how free from government regulation the market should be. Some argue that the best thing is for businesses to operate without intervention of any kind in a totally free-market economy, also known as a *laissez-faire* economy (from the French "let them do"). On the other hand, there are some who advocate complete government control over the exchange of goods in a centrally planned, or "command" economy. Karl Marx (see pp. 44–45) pointed out the unfairness of a market economy, which benefitted the capitalist owners of industry at the cost of the working class. In its place, he proposed a communist society, which as well as collectively owning the means of production (factories and mills), could plan the production and distribution of goods centrally, rather than leaving that to market forces.

> # IN ECONOMIC LIFE COMPETITION IS NEVER COMPLETELY LACKING, BUT HARDLY EVER IS IT PERFECT.
>
> **JOSEPH SCHUMPETER**

The middle ground

Marx's ideas of a planned economy were adopted by a number of communist states in the 20th century, with varying degrees of success. They were criticized by western economists, such as the Austro-Hungarian Ludwig von Mises, who argued that command economies could not respond to changes in supply and demand as quickly as the market, leading to huge surpluses and devastating shortages. Most economies operate between the two extremes. The influential English economist John Maynard Keynes (see pp. 106–07), while recognizing the strengths of competitive markets, argued that governments should intervene to lessen the effects of the economic ups and downs—especially in times of depression.

See also: 48–49, 52–53, 64–65 →

PROVIDING THE BEST PRODUCT AT THE BEST PRICE

Who's in CHARGE?

WITH THE ARRIVAL OF MANUFACTURING INDUSTRIES, ECONOMIC POWER SHIFTED AWAY FROM THE LANDOWNING ARISTOCRACY WHO HAD PROSPERED FROM THE AGRICULTURAL ECONOMY. NOW FACTORIES WERE OWNED AND RUN BY FAMILIES, INDIVIDUALS, OR PARTNERSHIPS. TODAY, MOST LARGE COMPANIES ARE JOINTLY OWNED BY A NUMBER OF SHAREHOLDERS AND RUN BY MANAGERS.

Joining together

The idea of joint ownership of a business had been around before the Industrial Revolution, when businesses got together to form companies to trade internationally. When manufacturing industries began producing goods on a large scale, it made sense for people to go into partnership to raise the necessary money, and to share the profits. Of course, small businesses continued to exist, such as individual craftspeople and store owners or people employing a small workforce. Some even formed small private companies in which each person had a share of the business.

The large factories and mills mass-producing goods and employing large numbers of people often needed to raise considerable sums of money to finance their businesses, and offered shares in their companies to the public. By buying shares in public companies, known as corporations, investors provide the company with money to buy buildings and machinery, and to pay workers. In return, they receive a share of the profits, known as dividends. Shareholders are also given a say in how the business is run, normally through voting at meetings when the company directors are appointed.

KARL MARX

Marx was born in what is now Germany. He studied law and philosophy before becoming a journalist, but had to flee to Paris because of his socialist political views. There he met Friedrich Engels, and they wrote *The Communist Manifesto* in 1848. Marx moved to London, where he wrote *Das Kapital*, an analysis of capitalism and an explanation of his economic theory.

A share of the business ⬆

Large companies can be owned by a number of different investors, who buy shares in the company and have a say in how it is run.

It's good to share

However, shareholders actually have little control over the day-to day running of the firm. The business is managed by a board of directors who have been appointed by the shareholders to make decisions on how it is run. Often, they are chosen for their abilities to make a profit for the shareholders, and have shares in the company themselves. The amount of say shareholders have in the business is in direct proportion to the number of shares they hold, so that if someone has more than 50 percent of the shares he or she effectively controls the company.

In practice, however, it is unusual for an individual person to have a majority shareholding in a major firm. In large companies, there are often many different kinds of shareholder, not just individual investors. Some shares are bought by investment companies, banks, and pension funds, some by the directors and workers in the company, and others by other companies or even governments.

The world's largest employer is the US Department of Defense, with over 3.2 million employees.

> **UNDER CAPITALISM, MAN EXPLOITS MAN, UNDER COMMUNISM, IT'S JUST THE OPPOSITE.**
> JOHN KENNETH GALBRAITH

Mixing it up

In a capitalist free-market economy, most companies are owned by private investors— individuals or companies—although the government may also hold some shares. But there are some industries in which the government often has a controlling interest, holding the majority of the shares, or owning the company. These nationalized industries, or state-owned enterprises, usually provide important facilities such as mail, health care, and public transportation, but also essential services such as the police and defense forces. Most countries today have some form of "mixed economy," with varying proportions of private and state-owned industries. This is as much for political as economic reasons, and demonstrates the key difference between capitalism (private ownership of capital) and socialism or communism (state ownership of the means of production).

See also: 42-43, 100-101

MANY PEOPLE CAN HAVE A SLICE OF ONE COMPANY.

PRIVATE COMPANIES

CAPITALIST OWNER

BOARD OF DIRECTORS

WORKERS' COOPERATIVE

SHAREHOLDERS

FROM SUPPLIER TO CONSUMER

SUPPLIER OF RAW MATERIAL

MANUFACTURER OF GOODS

How businesses

FROM THE CUSTOMER'S POINT OF VIEW, BUSINESSES EXIST TO PROVIDE THE GOODS AND SERVICES THEY NEED AND WANT. BUT FOR THE OWNERS AND MANAGERS OF THOSE BUSINESSES THAT IS ONLY HALF THE STORY. THEY PRODUCE THOSE GOODS AND SERVICES IN ORDER TO MAKE MONEY. TO DO THIS, THEIR BUSINESSES HAVE TO BE CAREFULLY MANAGED TO MAKE A PROFIT.

> **PROFIT OR PERISH... THERE ARE ONLY TWO WAYS TO MAKE MONEY: INCREASE SALES AND DECREASE COSTS.**
>
> FRED DELUCA, US BUSINESSMAN

Balancing the books

Businesses of all sorts, from individual traders, or small private companies to huge international corporations, make money for their owners or shareholders by selling their products. They may produce commodities, manufactured goods, or services, but all aim to be profitable. This means they are run so that there is more money coming into the business than is being spent. It is the task of the management, either the owners of a small firm or the managers in a large company, to balance the costs of production with the revenue—the money that comes from sales of the product. When income is greater than expenditure, the business makes a profit, but when expenditure is greater than income it makes a loss.

Money out and money in

Whoever is running a business has to consider the costs of production—the money that needs to be spent to make their product. If it is a manufacturing industry, for example, this will include the cost of raw materials that the product is made from—the paper and ink of a book, for example—the buildings and machinery needed to make it, and the wages of the workers. There may also be other costs, such as delivery of the goods to the customer, and payment for services including heating and lighting, repairs and maintenance of equipment, and insurance. If the business makes a profit, it will also have to pay some tax to the government. On the other side of the equation is the income a business gets from selling the product. Once a business is running successfully,

RETAILER OF PRODUCTS

CONSUMER

OPERATE

FROM THE SUPPLIER OF THE RAW MATERIALS TO THE SALE TO THE CONSUMER OF THE FINISHED PRODUCT, AT EACH STAGE BUSINESSES AIM TO MAKE A PROFIT.

this income can be used to pay for the costs of production. But starting a new business involves costs, such as buying machinery and paying for premises, before any goods can be produced and sold. Even established businesses need to spend money, from time to time, to increase production before they see a return on that money. So, in addition to revenue from sales, a business can raise money by taking a loan from the bank, or by selling shares in the company. In return, it will pay the bank interest on the loan, or the shareholders a share of the profit.

> The ratio of profit to income from the sales of a product is known as the "profit margin."

Making a profit
To ensure the best income from sales, the business should identify its market, those people most likely to want its products. Some businesses, especially in the service sector, sell their products directly to the consumer, but there are often many different businesses involved in getting a finished product to the customer. For example, raw materials are supplied to manufacturers, who in turn supply stores with their products, which they offer for sale to their customers— each selling to the other for a profit. Many small businesses are run by the people who own them,

but large companies employ qualified people as directors to manage the business. They ensure that the business is profitable, and decide what products to make and how they are sold. Due to pressure from shareholders to make a quick profit, they sometimes focus on this rather than reinvesting profit to improve productivity or working conditions. Managers may be tempted to run companies for their own gain rather than the long-term good of the company.

See also: 52–53, 56–57

STICK AND CARROT
Managers must ensure that their employees are working for the good of the business. Management expert Douglas McGregor identified two basic styles of management, Theory X and Theory Y: either threatening the workers with punishment if their work is not good enough, or rewarding them for good work.

Running an BUSINESS

See also: 50–51

IN ORDER TO SUCCEED IN A FREE MARKET, BUSINESSES NEED TO OFFER THEIR PRODUCTS AT COMPETITIVE PRICES. THE PRODUCTIVITY OF A BUSINESS—HOW EFFICIENTLY IT PRODUCES ITS GOODS OR SERVICES—IS KEY TO SUCCESS. GOOD MANAGERS ENSURE THAT PRODUCTION COSTS ARE KEPT TO A MINIMUM.

One job at a time

Managers are always looking for ways to increase productivity, which is the ratio of costs to output in production. Adam Smith, writing when the manufacturing industry was new, described a way that production could be made more efficient, known as

> THE GREATEST **IMPROVEMENT** IN THE **PRODUCTIVE** POWERS OF LABOR... SEEMS TO HAVE BEEN THE EFFECTS OF THE **DIVISION OF LABOR.**
>
> ADAM SMITH

the "division of labor." Making most manufactured goods involves several different processes using different skills. Smith's example was the manufacture of pins: the wire is straightened, sharpened, a head is put on, and then it is polished. One worker could do all these tasks, and make 20 pins in a day. But this work can be divided into its separate processes, with a number of workers each performing one task. Because each worker specializes in one job, he or she can work much faster without changing from one task to another. Now 10 workers can produce thousands of pins in a day—a huge increase in productivity from the 200 they would have produced before.

WHEN EACH WORKER IS GIVEN A SPECIFIC TASK...

efficient

Scale it up

Another way of increasing productivity comes from economies of scale. The more goods a factory produces, the cheaper it is to make each item. This is because fixed costs, for things such as the buildings and machinery, must be paid whatever the output of the factory. So if a large quantity of goods is made the costs are spread over a larger number of items. Costs are also reduced by buying raw materials in bulk.

Another production cost is labor. Machines can now do many jobs, and a single machine can often do the work of many people using only one operative. This is why businesses spend some of their profits on research and development, looking for ways to improve the efficiency of their equipment. Labor can be cheaper in poor countries, so businesses in richer countries may outsource production abroad.

Tougher cuts

Improving productivity in the service industry is harder because it largely relies on human resources. Information technology, however, has brought some changes. For example, businesses no longer have to be based in expensive cities, and services can be done via the internet or by email.

Businesses that focus on producing high-quality goods emphasize the fact that they are handmade in a traditional way. These businesses thrive because of a demand for quality products for which customers will pay higher prices. These prices cover the higher production costs.

> Shipbuilders in Venice, Italy, developed assembly-line methods in the 14th century.

ASSEMBLY LINES

In factories, workers may be engaged at different stages of the production process. The product is passed from one work station to the next on an assembly line, which is more efficient than workers moving around with their tools. By 1913 assembly lines on conveyor belts had appeared, and were used for mass-producing Ford's Model T automobile.

➋ Many hands

By having each worker focus on just one aspect of production, rather than changing from one task to another, productivity is increased greatly.

THE MANUFACTURING PROCESS IS MORE EFFICIENT.

COOPERATIVE MOVEMENTS

COOPERATIVES INVOLVE PEOPLE SUCH AS
FARMERS OR CONSUMERS BANDING TOGETHER
TO CREATE AN ENTERPRISE IN WHICH ALL HAVE
AN EQUAL STAKE. BY DOING THIS, COOP MEMBERS
MEET THEIR NEEDS IN A WAY THEY COULDN'T ON
THEIR OWN. THIS WAY, THEY CAN ACHIEVE SOCIAL
BENEFITS WITHIN THE CAPITALIST ECONOMY.

BANKS AND CREDIT UNIONS

Credit unions are, in effect, small, private
banks run by the people who bank with
them. They help members come together
to save and take out loans at fair rates.
Most are open only to people who share
an interest such as a profession or
religion. Cooperative banks are larger
and differ from commercial banks only
in that they are owned by their customers
and often have ethical investment policies.

WORKER COOPERATIVES

A worker cooperative is a business owned by
its workers. There is no single owner,
and the workers run the business by and
for themselves. The business may be run
by all the members democratically or by an
elected management. A worker coop, some
people argue, is the natural alternative to
businesses run purely for profit. Instead of
capital hiring workers, workers hire capital
and this gives the workers more control.

In the
Netherlands,
nearly a third
of all homes are
owned by
housing coops.

HOUSING COOPERATIVES

A housing cooperative owns and runs residential property on behalf of those who live there. By pooling resources, members of a housing coop can buy better housing and services than they could afford individually. When anyone leaves, the coop's management selects new residents on behalf of members. For many people, housing coops are the only way to get decent housing.

CONSUMER COOPERATIVES

A consumer coop is a business owned by its customers. By clubbing together, members gain the clout to get big savings from bulk purchasing, or cutting out profit-hungry retailers. The goal is to provide members with goods at the lowest price possible rather than offering them at the highest price shoppers will pay in order to maximize profits. The UK's Cooperative Group is the world's largest consumer coop, comprising stores, insurance, travel, funeral, and banking services.

⬆ **Working together**
When individuals come together to form a cooperative movement they can use their strength of numbers to negotiate a better deal for their members.

> "**Cooperatives** are a **reminder** to the international community that it is possible to pursue both **economic viability** and **social responsibility.**"
>
> BAN Ki-MOON, SECRETARY-GENERAL OF THE UNITED NATIONS

Going to **WORK**

EVERY INDUSTRY NEEDS LABOR. MANUFACTURING, CONSTRUCTION, FARMING, AND ESPECIALLY THE SERVICE INDUSTRIES ALL NEED WORKERS TO PRODUCE GOODS AND PERFORM SERVICES. JUST LIKE OTHER RESOURCES, LABOR IS BOUGHT AND SOLD AS WORKERS OFFER THEIR TIME AND SKILLS, AND EMPLOYERS PAY FOR IT WITH WAGES AND SALARIES.

See also: 50–51, 126–127

Pricing the job

All businesses, other than one-person businesses and partnerships, need to employ workers. And most people need some kind of employment to earn the money to live on. This provides both supply and demand—employers supply jobs and have a demand for human resources, or labor, and workers supply their labor and have a demand for jobs. The way businesses and workforce interact is known as the "labor market." As in other markets, supply and demand determine price, in this case the price of labor, or the amount paid in wages or salaries. Employers naturally want to minimize their costs, so they try to keep wages down, while workers negotiate for the highest wages they can. But if there is a plentiful supply of labor, as with any commodity, the price will fall, and employers can pay lower wages when there are a lot of workers looking for jobs. This is often the case with unskilled labor, especially in places with large populations. On the other hand, workers with a particular skill are often scarce, and businesses pay more to employ them.

A working balance

The labor market is a way of allocating human resources, distributing jobs to the workers, and providing employers with the people they need to conduct their business. In an ideal world, with a perfect labor market, both sides would benefit. But in practice, neither labor nor jobs are perfectly distributed. Some countries

WORKER'S RIGHTS

Employers sometimes force their workers to accept low wages and work long hours. To protect themselves from exploitation, workers form trade unions. The unions enable workers to negotiate collectively with employers about their working conditions, using the ultimate threat of withdrawing their labor—a strike—as a bargaining tool.

MECHANIC

$25,000

have a large unskilled workforce with not enough jobs to go around, and a lack of workers with the necessary skills to fill other vacancies. In this case, employers may have to pay out more to train workers. In some rich countries, there is the opposite problem, where the workforce is highly skilled, and there are not enough skilled job vacancies. Skilled workers may then have to consider taking lower-paid, unskilled work.

Out of work
Another result of the uneven distribution of jobs and workers, which has many causes, is unemployment. Some jobs are seasonal, for example, in the tourist industry, and workers may lose their jobs during slack periods. Or it may be due to overproduction, when a business has a surplus of goods and no longer needs workers to produce them—or when there is a fall in demand for goods, such as television sets or calculators that become outdated. Mechanization in many industries also

> **ECONOMICS IS EXTREMELY USEFUL AS A FORM OF EMPLOYMENT FOR ECONOMISTS.**
> JOHN KENNETH GALBRAITH

puts people out of work. At any one time, there are a number of people who are able and willing to work, but can't find a job. The unemployment rates—the percentage of the working age population out of work—varies, and is seen as an indication of a country's economic prosperity. But these rates give only an overall picture, indicating that more people want to work than there are jobs available. What they don't show is how many people are between jobs or working in a seasonal industry, and how many are out of work long-term. Nor do the rates explain a mismatch between the skills of the workforce and those needed for the available jobs.

> **Unemployment rates among young people (ages 16—28) are much higher than rates among adults.**

⊙ The rate for the job
In an ideal labor market, workers looking for a job bring the skills required by employers. Highly skilled workers, or those with skills that are scarce, can demand more money for their labor.

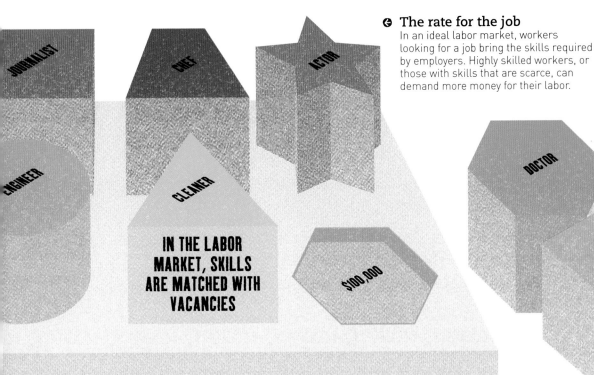

IN THE LABOR MARKET, SKILLS ARE MATCHED WITH VACANCIES

Big SPENDERS

SUPPLIERS COULDN'T EXIST IF CUSTOMERS DIDN'T WANT TO BUY, OR CONSUME, THEIR GOODS AND SERVICES. IN RICHER COUNTRIES, WHERE PEOPLE HAVE MORE MONEY TO SPEND ON LUXURIES, CONSUMERS ARE CONTINUALLY BEING URGED TO BUY THINGS, IN WHAT HAS BECOME KNOWN AS THE "CONSUMER SOCIETY."

Boom time

In addition to changing the way we make goods, the manufacturing industries that emerged during the Industrial Revolution in the late 18th century altered almost every aspect of our lives. Industrialized societies prospered, especially the new class of capitalists, the mill and factory owners, whose goods supplied an increasing number of stores. But these goods need buyers. Much of the wealth went to the business owners, while the workers earned wages from their jobs in the new industries. There were now more people, especially in towns and cities, needing to buy necessities, and an increasing number of rich businesspeople wanting to buy luxury goods. The market—the supply and demand for these goods— grew. Production increased in line with demand, and the economy of industrial societies flourished as industries supplied ever more manufactured goods and found ways of producing them more efficiently. Increased demand drove down prices of everyday goods, as producers vied for business.

Shopping spree

As industrialized societies prospered, so too did the retail sector—the shops and stores selling goods to the public. In industrial towns and cities, rather than visiting the rural farmers' markets, the workers and owners of the factories bought their goods from local shops. The centers of many urban areas soon became shopping districts, and today many have developed into indoor shopping malls. The retail industry has also continued to grow, alongside manufacturing, as people have more money to spend. Many of the individual retail businesses have grown into large department stores or supermarkets offering a range of different products, or into chain stores with branches in many towns. Today, in richer countries, there are also out-of-town superstores and

Covering 12.1 million sq ft (1,124,000 m²) and with 1,200 retail outlets, the Dubai Mall is the world's largest shopping mall.

Spend, spend, spend
As people become more prosperous, they have more money to spare after paying for necessities. They are encouraged to spend this on consumer goods.

> CONSUMPTION IS THE SOLE END AND PURPOSE OF ALL PRODUCTION.
> ADAM SMITH

shopping malls. Retail is now major business, employing huge numbers of people. It relies on customers, so competing retailers encourage consumers to buy their products. Because we are all potential customers, we are continually being urged to consume and spend more, and this emphasis on consumption rather than production of goods is often referred to as "consumerism." To do this, retailers have made shopping easier, by offering telephone and online purchasing, or presenting shopping as a pleasurable activity rather than a chore.

SHOWING OFF

Most goods we buy are needed or are things to make life easier. But economist Thorstein Veblen noticed that people buy some goods as status symbols, to show off how much money they have to spend. These examples of conspicuous consumption, such as a Rolls Royce, are known as "Veblen goods."

GIORGIO ARMANI

Life's little luxuries

In rich countries, more people have money to spare after buying the essentials and can afford to spend on things they want, rather than need. In addition to buying goods that give them pleasure, people spend money on services. These include things like laundry and cleaning, or hairdressing and beauty treatments, that previously they would have done for themselves. As a result, people also have more leisure time, which they can enjoy following their interests or relaxing. This means that they can spend money on leisure activities—for example, going on vacation or buying music, books, or computer games.

SHOPPING FOR THINGS WE DON'T REALLY NEED HAS BECOME A LEISURE ACTIVITY

See also: 36–37, 130–131

TIME OFF

Technology now does much of our work for us, offering a chance for us all to have more leisure time. But in fact it's put many people out of work, while others are working just as hard because they can't afford to work fewer hours if it means less pay. There's less work, but more people chasing it.

LOSS LEADERS

One way of attracting customers is with special offers. Supermarkets, for example, may offer goods at less than cost price. These "loss leaders," as they are called, bring in people who may buy other things while they're in the store. Other businesses offer introductory deals but lock in customers on long-term contracts, which may not be such a good deal.

Resources and businesses
IN PRACTICE

SERVICE SOCIETY

Towns and cities in developed countries have offices, stores, and restaurants but little of the industrial past is visible. In these places, it's easy to imagine a "postindustrial society" based on services alone. But, we will always need industry to supply manufactured goods and agriculture to supply food.

WHERE IN THE WORLD

Natural resources are plentiful in some places in the world and scarce in others. For example, in some countries water is freely available, but in others it's valuable enough for people to fight over. Control of resources such as oil or minerals, gives countries political clout.

Competition pushes producers to offer better products at lower prices. But while consumers have more choice of products to buy, there's often a confusingly large number of very similar products. Faced with too many alternatives, with only slight differences, consumers find it difficult to make a good choice.

TOO MUCH CHOICE

KEEPING UP-TO-DATE

Technology is advancing faster than ever, and producers are continually trying to persuade us to buy their latest products. Electronic goods in particular become obsolete fast, so last year's expensive smartphone, even if it still works perfectly, becomes worth next to nothing once technology has moved on.

We as consumers buy our goods and services from suppliers, who offer them for sale in the market. The products that are offered, and their price, depends on the demand for them. This in turn determines the way that we use our resources, who gets what, and the sorts of industry that we have.

In the face of competition from large corporations, many smaller firms have gone out of business or been bought up by larger firms. Some companies have grown so big that they are richer than many countries, and governments can't afford to ignore them.

THE BIG BOYS

A NICHE IN THE MARKET

When starting up a business or launching a new product, it's important to be competitive. It isn't enough simply to have a good product, especially if someone else is already selling something similar. To find a place in the market, your product needs to satisfy a demand that isn't already being met. This is known as filling a niche in the market.

Does **MONEY** make the world go round?

Let WELL ENOUGH ALONE

Free TRADE

It's a SMALL world

Economic UPS and DOWNS

When markets don't DO THEIR JOB

A TAXING problem

What does the FUTURE hold?

A RISKY business

An informed GAMBLE

Is GREED good?

Making the right DECISION

Costing the EARTH

Countries have traded with one another for thousands of years, but today modern transportation and communications mean that international trade is an important part of every country's economy. Globalization means that there are now many companies selling and even producing their goods abroad. This has brought prosperity to many parts of the world, but the worldwide spread of industry has also brought serious environmental problems.

Let well enough ALONE

IN A MARKET, SUPPLY AND DEMAND ARE MATCHED SO BOTH PRODUCERS
AND CONSUMERS BENEFIT. THIS WORKS IN THEORY, BUT IN PRACTICE THE
SYSTEM IS NOT PERFECT. MARKETS NEED REGULATION TO MAKE SURE
THAT SOME PEOPLE DO NOT BENEFIT MORE THAN OTHERS.

Perfectly balanced

In an ideal world, the way that buyers and sellers
reach deals in the market would lead to a perfect
balance of supply and demand. Left to its own
devices, the market would regulate itself. But in
reality this doesn't always happen. Economists have
different views on how much markets should be left
alone, and how much there should be some control
over the way they operate. At one extreme, *laissez-
faire* economists argue for completely free markets
with no intervention, and at the other, Marxian
economists—those who follow the theories of Karl
Marx (see p. 48)—argue for complete government
control over production. Between these extremes,
the mainstream of economic thinkers agrees that
there have to be some regulations to compensate
for the failings of the market system, with some

**SUPPLY CREATES ITS
OWN DEMAND.**
JOHN MAYNARD KEYNES

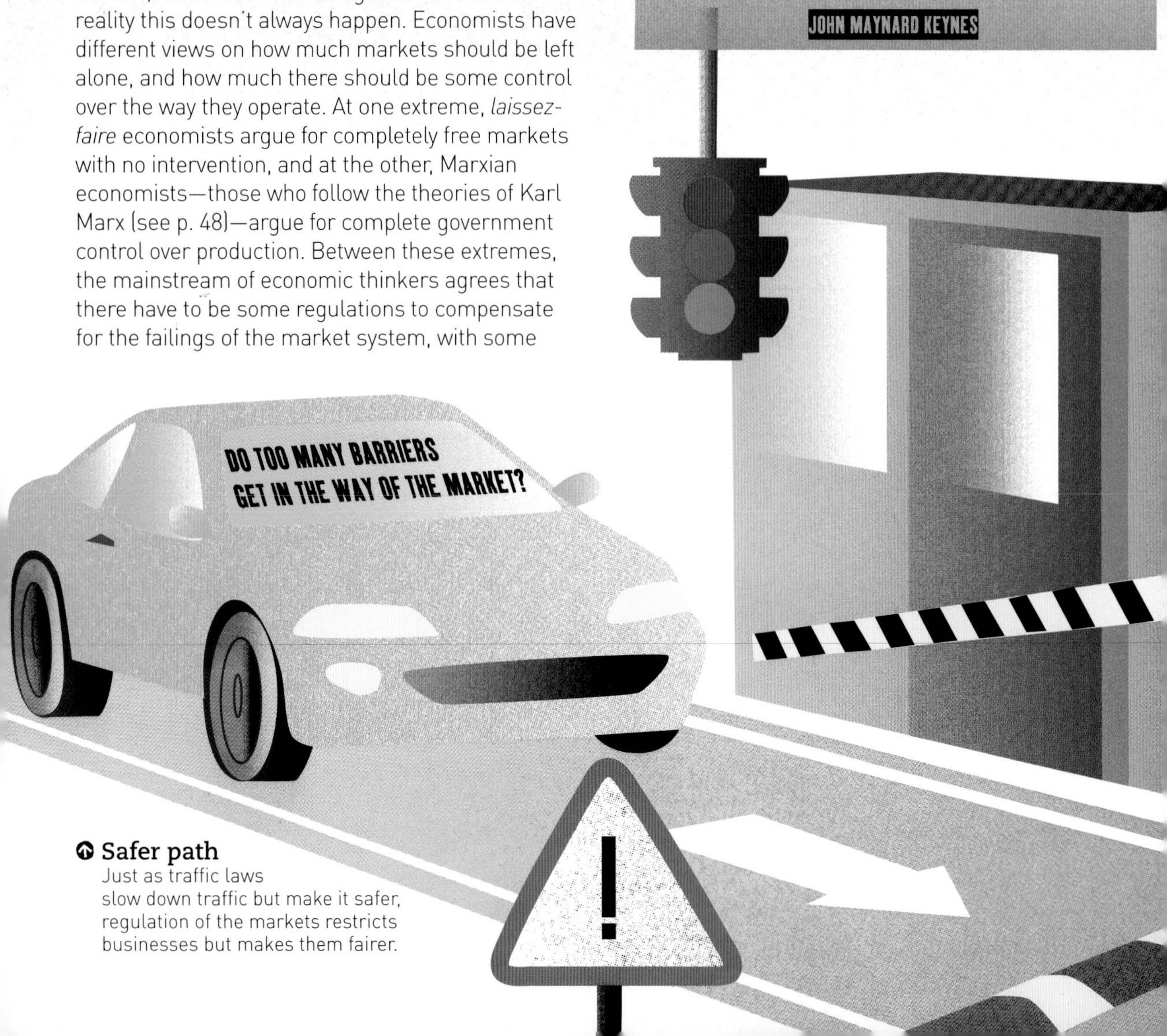

DO TOO MANY BARRIERS
GET IN THE WAY OF THE MARKET?

⬆ **Safer path**
Just as traffic laws
slow down traffic but make it safer,
regulation of the markets restricts
businesses but makes them fairer.

government intervention. Where they may disagree, however, is about just how free markets should be, and how much governments should intervene.

Free thinkers

Free-market economists say that most regulation is unnecessary; it gets in the way of businesses helping the economy to grow and discourages innovation. It's true that some laws restrict what businesses can do, but no one would object to laws that stop someone from offering his services as a hit man or selling addictive drugs. And some regulations imposed on businesses are designed to prevent criminal activities such as fraud and bribery, or the sale of faulty goods.

Businesses naturally want the freedom to act in their own best interests, or for the good of their companies and shareholders, but governments must act in the interest of the public, and the economy of the country as a whole. For instance, businesses see

taxes as a burden, even though they provide governments with the money to sustain public services such as education and health care for those who couldn't afford to pay for them. In many countries, there are laws against unfair trading practices to protect the rights of consumers and to ensure workers get fair pay and working conditions.

Some economists believe governments should intervene to help the country's economy. One of the downsides of a free market is that it has spells of boom and bust. If a government has some control over the planning of its economy, it can minimize these fluctuations and maybe avoid a financial crisis. Some government intervention, such as taxes on imported goods, and subsidies for industries to help them to compete with foreign companies, can be beneficial to businesses, too.

Free or equal?

The arguments for and against free markets or government intervention are not purely economic. They are based on politics, too. The choice boils down to freedom versus equality. Unregulated markets, favored by liberal countries, allow people the freedom to choose, but at the price of an unequal society; while centrally controlled economies, advocated by socialist politicians and economists, offer a fairer distribution of wealth but more restrictions. Even in "mixed economies" the balance changes over time, so that since the 1980s, a *laissez-faire* approach has tended to dominate in many countries around the world.

See also: 14–15, 32–33, 38–39

North Korea, a socialist state, is the most centrally planned economy in the world.

A FAILED EXPERIMENT?

During the 20th century, many countries adopted some form of communist government that controlled production of goods and services. In most cases, these centrally governed economies failed to match the demand, and there was overproduction of some goods and a shortage of others. Most economists regard the failure of these economies as proof of the necessity of free markets.

Free TRADE

AS WELL AS GOODS AND SERVICES THAT ARE PRODUCED AND SOLD WITHIN A COUNTRY, THERE ARE SOME THAT ARE PRODUCED FOR SALE IN OTHER COUNTRIES, AND OTHERS BOUGHT FROM ABROAD. FOR THOUSANDS OF YEARS, COUNTRIES HAVE TRADED WITH ONE ANOTHER, IMPORTING GOODS THAT ARE SCARCE AT HOME AND EXPORTING THOSE IN DEMAND ELSEWHERE.

See also: 32–33, 48–49

What's needed where

Within a country, there is trade between the producers of different kinds of goods, to ensure that they are distributed to where they are needed. For example, people need to have food transported into towns and cities from farming areas, and those living in the country require manufactured goods produced in industrial areas. The same is true across the world. Some countries, for example, have the right climate for growing certain crops, while others have different natural resources such as oil or minerals, or have developed a skill in making certain kinds of goods. By trading with one another, countries exchange goods they produce for those that they need. This kind of international trade began with ancient civilizations and became an important part of many countries' economies as trade routes were established to transport goods around the world. Before the Industrial Revolution (see pp. 42–43), major businesses were run by merchants, international traders, rather than producers of goods.

> The Silk Road was a trade route linking China, India, Arabia, and Europe for more than 1,500 years.

● Food for goods

If a country is good at farming but not at manufacturing, it may produce enough food to feed its own people and to export to other countries, and choose to import goods such as cars.

Play to your strengths

Since the growth of manufacturing industries, international trade has continued to play an essential part of

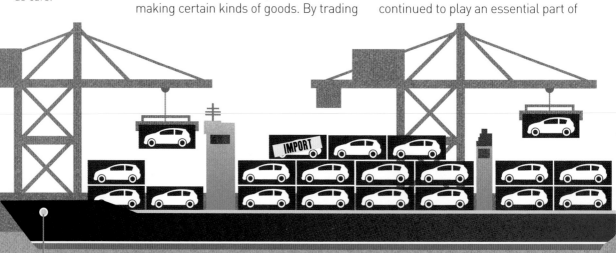

PRODUCE IS EXPORTED FOR GOODS THAT ARE NEEDED

every country's economy. In most cases, it is practically impossible for a country to be entirely self-sufficient, as it may not have the resources to produce some of the goods that its people need. These have to be imported from elsewhere, in exchange for money, or goods that the other country needs. But it's not always the case that a country can't produce the necessary goods. Sometimes it's actually cheaper

DAVID RICARDO (1772–1823)

Born in London, Ricardo, like his father, was a stockbroker. After making a fortune buying government bonds before the Battle of Waterloo (1815), he became a politician. One of the foremost classical economists, he wrote *On the Principles of Political Economy and Taxation* in 1817.

> **... AN ECONOMIST'S CREED ... WOULD SURELY CONTAIN ... "I ADVOCATE FREE TRADE."**
> PAUL KRUGMAN, US ECONOMIST

to buy them from another country than make them at home. For example, a country that is mainly agricultural may be able to make manufactured goods such as cars, but have an auto industry that is small and not very efficient. But because its agriculture is productive, it can feed its own people and have enough to sell to another country. At the same time, the other country may be able to make cars more efficiently, keeping production costs low, yet not be able to produce enough food. It would be a mistake for the first country to try to make more cars, taking money and workers away from the

farming that it does well. In the words of economist David Ricardo (see panel above), that country has a "comparative advantage" in agriculture, and does far better to specialize in that.

Protect your assets

International trade is not always seen as a good thing. Exporting goods brings money in but imports must be paid for. If a country is in deficit, spending more on imports than it is receiving for exports, its government may try to restrict imports. It is often possible, for example, to produce the same goods locally, but not as cheaply. To protect producers in their own countries from foreign competition, some governments impose tariffs, which are taxes on imported goods, to make them more expensive. Some economists disagree with this kind of "protectionism," as it is called. They argue that there should be free international trade without government restrictions.

See also: 68–69, 104–105

EXPORT

It's a SMALL

See also: 34–35, 52–53, 66–67

INTERNATIONAL TRADE HAS EXISTED FOR AS LONG AS THERE HAVE BEEN NATIONS. FIRST, IT WAS BETWEEN NEIGHBORING COUNTRIES, THEN IT SPREAD ACROSS THE WORLD AS SHIPS, RAILROADS, ROADS, AND PLANES MADE TRANSPORTING GOODS EASIER. CHEAP, RELIABLE TRANSPORTATION AND COMMUNICATIONS NOW MEAN BUSINESSES CAN BE TRULY GLOBAL.

A bigger marketplace

There are around 200 different countries in the world today, and with modern transportation it's possible to travel to any of them, and communicate with them by phone or via the internet. Businesses producing goods and services for export now have many more potential customers than ever before, in what's effectively a global marketplace. In the same way that market economies have developed within each country, so too a global market economy is emerging. The idea that a free market, with some government regulation, is the most efficient way of matching the supply and demand of goods and services also applies to globalized trade. Countries trade with one another to their mutual benefit, and competition between them ensures their businesses are productive and prices are fair. But, like any other market, there are in practice some restrictions. Some countries, for example, impose import taxes on certain goods or ban trade with certain countries. Others have joined together to form free trade areas that will trade with each other, but have strict regulations about trading with the rest of the world.

COMPANIES CAN OPERATE ALL OVER THE WORLD

HEADQUARTERS

SUBSIDIARY COMPANIES

❷ Global business

Large companies tend to have their headquarters in rich countries but often produce goods in poorer, developing countries to save on transportation and labor costs.

World

Going global

In general, there has been a steady trend toward globalization, with increasingly free trade worldwide. Big companies have taken advantage of the opportunity to sell their products to different countries, and many now have customers all over the world. Some firms such as supermarket chains or fast-food restaurants have opened outlets in other countries to sell their goods or services.

There are also large corporations that not only sell their products abroad, but also produce the goods in other countries. These so-called transnational, or multinational, companies are generally based in rich, developed countries where they have their headquarters. Although the company is owned and managed from here, it may produce little or none of the goods in its home country. There are several advantages to locating production facilities in another country. For example, shipping costs can be reduced if the goods are manufactured in the country that is going to buy them. The cost of importing raw materials can also be avoided if factories are built in the country where they are produced. But the biggest saving is possibly on the workforce because it's almost always much cheaper to run a factory in a poorer, developing country, where labor costs are lower.

WHEN AMERICA SNEEZES, THE **WHOLE WORLD** CATCHES A **COLD**.

ANON

The Dutch East India Company, established in 1602, is considered the first modern multinational corporation.

Who profits?

Today, multinational corporations produce goods in many different countries, and sell their goods around the world. The value of the trade is often more than that of a whole country. The scope of the business may be global, they may employ people in various countries, but a US-based multinational, for example, is likely to have its management and shareholders based in the US, too, and that's where the company's profits will be directed.

See also: 104–05, 110–11

MOVEMENT OF LABOR

Globalization evolved through international trade, which relies on goods moving freely between countries. While this has become more widespread, the same isn't true of the movement of labor, allowing people to move from one country to another to work. Many countries restrict immigration to protect jobs for their workforce, but others argue that immigrant labor is vital to the economy.

Economic UPS and DOWNS

See also: 50–51, 126–127

PEOPLE IN INDUSTRIALIZED COUNTRIES HAVE SEEN THEIR STANDARD OF LIVING DRAMATICALLY IMPROVE OVER THE LAST 200 YEARS. THIS IS THE RESULT OF ECONOMIC GROWTH, A GRADUAL INCREASE IN THE WEALTH OF A COUNTRY, ONE OF THE BENEFITS OF THE MARKET ECONOMY. BUT THIS GROWTH IS NOT A STEADY PROCESS, IT IS MARKED BY ECONOMIC UPS AND DOWNS.

> ANYONE WHO BELIEVES **EXPONENTIAL GROWTH** CAN GO ON FOREVER IN A **FINITE WORLD** IS EITHER A **MADMAN OR AN ECONOMIST.**
>
> KENNETH BOULDING, BRITISH ECONOMIST

Losing the balance

In an ideal world, with a "perfect" market, the quantity of the goods and services supplied would always balance the demand for them. But in practice, this market equilibrium, as it's called, isn't a steady state. There are many things outside the market that affect the levels of supply and demand. For example, an ice-cream seller may sell out if the weather's hot, but find few customers during a cold winter. Or demand for a product can vanish because of new technology, such as when the latest smartphone model is released and other producers can't sell their outdated versions.

So, there are continually changes in market activity. Generally, these are only small fluctuations from the equilibrium, but from time to time, there

> Slowing economic activity is called a "recession," but if it continues for a long time it is known as a "depression."

Economic activity in a market is not steady, but has ups and downs. Circumstances outside the market can effect supply and demand, leading to periods of growth and decline.

are periods when businesses are doing well, and the market grows, and others when the mismatch between supply and demand leads to a downturn in business. Though these ups and downs don't follow a pattern but reflect changing circumstances, this is called the business cycle. Rather than being balanced, economic activity—the amount of trading in the market—is always going up and down. Periods of growth and expansion switch with spells of decline or recession. In general, the trend of markets is one of gradual expansion—economic growth—with both supply and demand increasing and creating a better standard of living. But there are times when this economic growth snowballs, causing an economic "boom." And there are times when it slows, or even declines, leading to economic recession.

Boom and bust

The instability of market economies, which alternate between "boom and bust," is a major disadvantage, even if in the long term they provide economic growth. It's the main reason given for government regulation of free markets.

Until recently, most economists believed that, even though there are ups and downs, market economies can keep growing and improving living standards. This idea was first put forward when populations were much smaller, and

it seemed we could go on using more natural resources indefinitely. However, environmentalists have made us aware that we live in a world of finite resources, which can't be replaced.

As economies grow, so we consume more resources. The supply of things we need to sustain growth is dwindling, and at the same time populations are increasing and demanding a better standard of living. In addition to becoming scarcer, our use of some resources, like fossil fuels such as oil, gas, and coal, is causing environmental problems that will have serious economic consequences. The continual improvement in our standard of living that we have enjoyed over the past two centuries cannot carry on, according to environmental economists. Instead of expecting continuous economic growth, we must achieve sustainable economies by reducing consumption and using renewable resources.

ECONOMIC GROWTH CAN BE A REAL ROLLER-COASTER RIDE OF HIGHS AND LOWS

THE WALL STREET CRASH

A dramatic example of boom and bust in the 20th century was the the Wall Street Crash. In the 1920s, business was booming in the stock market on Wall Street in New York, reflecting America's growing economy. But the situation changed sharply in 1929 when companies crashed, marking the start of the Great Depression that continued for the next decade.

ECONOMIC BUBBLES

AN ECONOMIC BUBBLE IS A MOMENT OF MARKET MADNESS. PEOPLE RUSH TO BUY SHARES IN WHAT SEEMS TO BE THE NEXT BIG THING. PRICES SOAR AS WORD SPREADS AND PEOPLE BUY IN. AFTER A TIME, PRICES GET SO HIGH THAT SOME INVESTORS LOSE THEIR NERVE AND PULL OUT. AS CONFIDENCE FAILS, PRICES CRASH, AND THE BUBBLE BURSTS.

TULIPOMANIA

In the 1630s, the Dutch middle classes went crazy over tulips, creating the first known economic bubble. It began when tulips from Turkey, with their vibrant colors, were found to thrive in Dutch gardens. Quickly, they became the must-have item for every well-to-do family, and bulbs were changing hands for sky-high prices. Then one day, a buyer refused to pay the price for a bulb at auction, and the tulip bubble burst and fortunes were lost.

SOUTH SEA BUBBLE

Economic bubbles got their name from a crash in 1720. The British parliament gave the South Sea Company a seemingly valuable monopoly on trade with South America in return for a loan. The company's shares soared, making investors apparently rich. Other schemes were quickly launched. But trade with South America went nowhere, and as many schemes came to nothing, stocks crashed.

⬇ When the bubble bursts

Economic bubbles form when there is a rush to buy shares in businesses producing a particular product or service. The market becomes overheated and investors begin to pull out, the bubble bursts, and prices fall dramatically.

HERD MENTALITY

In 1841, Scottish journalist Charles Mackay argued that economic bubbles are caused by "herd mentality." This is the idea that people can get swept up by how others behave, like a herd of buffalo stampeding. To predict when economic bubbles might happen, behavioral economists and psychologists like Daniel Kahneman study herd behavior to see how emotions such as greed and fear may drive stock markets.

> "Men, it has been well said, **think in herds**; it will be seen that they **go mad in herds,** while they only **recover** their senses slowly, and **one by one.**"

CHARLES MACKAY, SCOTTISH AUTHOR OF "EXTRAORDINARY POPULAR DELUSIONS AND THE MADNESS OF CROWDS"

DOTCOM BUBBLE

This century began with the bursting of the "dotcom" bubble. Convinced that the internet was going to change the way business was done overnight, speculators rushed to buy shares in new e-commerce companies. Some companies with no trading history and little income attracted billions of dollars of investment and share prices soared. But the values were all an illusion. The bubble burst and share prices plummeted catastrophically.

From 2000–02, 7 trillion dollars of investment in internet businesses was wiped out.

When markets
DO THEIR JOB

A MARKET IS GENERALLY CONSIDERED A GOOD WAY OF DISTRIBUTING GOODS AND SERVICES TO THE PEOPLE THAT NEED AND WANT THEM. SUPPLIERS OFFER THEM FOR SALE, AND CONSUMERS BUY THEM—AND EVERYONE BENEFITS FROM THE TRANSACTION. BUT MARKETS DON'T ALWAYS WORK THAT EFFICIENTLY.

> **CLIMATE CHANGE REPRESENTS THE GREATEST AND WIDEST-RANGING MARKET FAILURE EVER SEEN.**
> NICHOLAS STERN, BRITISH ECONOMIST

See also: 34–35, 48–49, 66–67

PUBLIC GOODS, SUCH AS FIREWORK DISPLAYS, ARE NOT SUPPLIED BY MARKETS

An unfair match

There are several ways that a market may fail to allocate goods and services as it is supposed to. Market failures are inevitable in free markets. Even the economists who argue that markets should be free to do their job without government interference and regulation recognize that, in practice, this isn't always possible.

One problem is that the two sides of a transaction, the buyer and the seller, may not always be evenly matched. The seller may have information about the goods that the buyer doesn't know about. Somebody who's selling a secondhand car, for example, may know that it will soon need expensive repairs, but is unlikely to say in case the buyer decides not to go ahead, or offers less money. Sometimes a buyer has the upper hand. Someone buying a run-down farm may get it for less than its worth because the owner doesn't know that a survey shows it's sitting on a huge oil field. This

"asymmetrical information," or unfairness, exists in all sorts of markets, and it would be odd to think that people wouldn't take advantage of it. To make the market fairer, governments often impose regulations about the disclosure of information, and laws to prevent "insider trading," using information that isn't available to the general public.

Total domination

A different form of unfairness comes from a lack of competition in a market. A monopoly, when there is only one seller

PAY HERE

don't

Free riding →

Because a firework display can be seen for miles around, people who have not paid to attend the event in a park can "free-ride" at the expense of those who have.

of a certain good, means that the buyer has no choice at all and is forced to pay whatever price the seller asks. Even if there are several suppliers of that good, they can join together in a group known as a cartel and agree not to compete on prices. Buyers then have to pay more than they would like, and the sellers can make an unfair profit at their expense.

Who will pay?

But not all market failures are so obvious. Both buyer and seller may be satisfied with their transaction, but at the expense of somebody else. When a transaction results in cost or harm to people who aren't involved in it, it's known as "an externality." If, for example, you buy an electric guitar and amplifier, you may be happy with the deal, and the store you bought it from has made a profit. But your family, and the neighbors, may suffer from the noise you're going to make. On a larger scale, businesses can produce the goods that consumers demand, and they may both benefit from this, but the pollution from the company's factory has to be cleaned up, generally at the public expense. There is a further kind of market failure that involves public

expense. There are some goods that it is difficult to prevent people from using for free. If you put on a firework display, for instance, the show will be in the sky where everyone can see it. It may be difficult to ask all the people who enjoy the fireworks to buy tickets for the event, so it is hard to get back the money spent buying the fireworks. This problem is called "free-riding" and it means that public goods such as street lighting, roads, and lighthouses are provided by governments rather than commercial enterprises.

Caveat emptor is Latin for "Let the buyer beware."

STATE SUBSIDIES

In most countries, governments provide public goods with money from taxpayers, or through state-owned companies. Or, they may give money to a business, as a subsidy, to encourage it to supply goods and services, such as clean energy, that would not otherwise make a profit.

See also: 44–45, 48–49

A **TAXING** problem

GOVERNMENTS ARE EXPECTED TO LOOK AFTER THE PEOPLE OF THEIR COUNTRY, PROVIDING SERVICES SUCH AS DEFENSE AND EDUCATION. THEY NEED MONEY TO PAY FOR THESE, AND THIS COMES FROM THE PEOPLE IN THE FORM OF TAXES. THE GOVERNMENT OF EACH COUNTRY DECIDES HOW MUCH TAX THEIR CITIZENS SHOULD PAY.

TAXES PAY FOR DEFENSE, POLICING, EDUCATION, HEALTH CARE, WELFARE, INFRASTRUCTURE, AND OVERSEAS AID

WAGES AND SALARIES

$

What's in it for me?

Almost everyone pays taxes in some form or another. It's the way in which we each make a contribution toward paying for things that benefit us all, and that we believe should be provided by the community as a whole. Perhaps most importantly, the money from taxes pays for the armed forces that protect our countries from enemies, and police forces to protect us from criminals. But there are many other services provided by the state that have to be paid for with public money. These include emergency services such as firefighters, as well as schools and hospitals. Our taxes may also be used to

⊖ Paying your taxes
A proportion of the money that we earn is paid in taxes to the government. This is used to provide public services that benefit society as a whole.

THE HARDEST THING TO UNDERSTAND IN THE WORLD IS THE INCOME TAX.
ALBERT EINSTEIN, GERMAN-BORN PHYSICIST

pay for public goods, like roads and street lighting, which private businesses couldn't produce profitably. The range of goods and services provided by the state varies from country to country. Some governments spend a big chunk of the money raised from taxes on welfare, including benefits for the poor, disabled, and unemployed, and retirement for older people, or to provide health care for everyone. Others prefer to provide only essential services, to keep government spending, and taxes, to a minimum.

> The first progressive income tax was levied in Britain in 1799 by William Pitt the Younger, to fund the war with France.

Making it fair
Providing public goods and services is not the only reason to impose taxes. By taxing certain goods, governments influence the market. For example, a tax can be put on goods from an industry that pollutes the environment. Their goods then become more expensive, so the producer and buyers are pushed to find alternatives. Many governments also tax things like alcohol and tobacco, to encourage healthier lifestyles. Similarly, businesses producing things that are considered desirable, like renewable energy, may be given low rates of taxation.

There are different ways governments can raise revenue, the money taken in taxes. This can be a proportion of the money a person earns from work—income tax—or that a business takes in profits, paid directly to the government. Other forms of direct tax are based on the amount of property, or wealth, a person owns. Direct taxes such as income tax are often progressive, so that the more money a person has, the larger proportion of it he or she pays in tax. There is also indirect taxation, such as an amount added to the price of goods and services. These taxes are criticized as unfair, as they are regressive, poor people pay a bigger proportion of their income on sales taxes than rich people.

A heavy burden
While most people agree with the idea of paying toward public services, taxes are seen as a burden. Economists who favor free markets argue that everything but essential services can be provided by private businesses, and that high taxes interfere with the market. US economist Alex Laffer argued that since lower taxes encourage businesses, governments have more revenue than if they impose a high tax rate. More left-wing economists argue that markets need some form of regulation, and taxes remove some of the unfairness of a free market.

See also: 100–101, 118–119 →

TAX AVOIDANCE
There are laws to ensure everyone pays their fair share of taxes. Tax evasion, such as lying about your income, is illegal. But no one wants to pay more than they have to, and some find legal ways to avoid paying taxes. One of these ways is to register the headquarters of a business in a tax haven, a country that has very low tax rates.

IN THIS WORLD NOTHING CAN BE SAID TO BE CERTAIN, EXCEPT DEATH AND TAXES.
BENJAMIN FRANKLIN, US POLITICAL THEORIST

What does the

THE PRICES OF GOODS IN A MARKET GO UP AND DOWN, REFLECTING THE CHANGES IN SUPPLY AND DEMAND. NATURALLY, BUSINESSES NEEDING TO BUY COMMODITIES WANT TO BUY WHEN PRICES ARE LOW, BUT OFTEN HAVE TO ORDER SUPPLIES MONTHS IN ADVANCE. IF THEY PAY FOR THEM AT TODAY'S PRICE, THEY MAY LOSE OUT IF THE PRICE FALLS, OR GAIN IF IT RISES.

Place your bets

Commodities such as oil, metals, and wheat are bought and sold in commodity markets, where sellers and buyers agree on a price. An oil-drilling company, for example, agrees to supply crude oil to an oil refinery for a certain amount per barrel. But, unlike a street market where a shopper pays for goods and takes them home, the oil isn't actually there for the buyer to use right away. It may be in a different country, and may even still be in the ground. Nor does any money change hands at this point. The buyer simply promises to pay the agreed price for a certain quantity of oil at an agreed date in the future, and the seller promises to supply that amount at that price. The agreement they make is known as a forward contract, or just a "forward." Because the date that the deal is actually completed may be months away, both buyer and seller are betting on the future price of oil, whether it will go up, or down. Before the oil is delivered and paid for, the contract to supply the oil, or to buy it, can be sold to another seller or buyer. The buyer agrees to buy from whomever holds the contract to supply, and the seller to supply the oil to whomever owns the contract to buy. The two sides of the forward contract can change many times between the original agreement and its end date.

> The value of derivatives is often more than the value of the actual assets traded.

Promises, promises

As with anything that can be bought and sold, forward contracts are traded in a market, known as the "futures market." It's not the commodities that are being bought or sold, but a promise to supply or to pay for them. These promises derive their value from the commodities and are called derivatives.

Dealers in foreign exchange markets also make forward contracts agreeing to buy or sell currencies at a set exchange rate on a set date, and these can also be traded. Derivatives can be made from almost anything that is bought or sold, when there's a contract between buyer and seller.

WHEN A BUYER AND SELLER AGREE ON THE TERMS OF A FUTURE TRANSACTION

DERIVATIVES ARE FINANCIAL WEAPONS OF MASS DESTRUCTION.

WARREN BUFFET, AMERICAN BUSINESS MAGNATE AND INVESTOR

FUTURE hold?

THEY ARE BOTH TRYING TO PREDICT WHAT THE PRICE WILL ACTUALLY BE

Fingers crossed

Bizarrely, even the contracts between banks and people they lend money to are regarded as derivatives that can be bought and sold. Like a forward contract to buy or sell a commodity, the loan agreement is a contract to pay by a certain time. So, the bank can sell this debt owing to them as a "financial product." Derivatives themselves, because they are traded, also involve agreements between buyers and sellers, which can become derivatives of derivatives, in a market that is becoming ever more complex. But even though the buying and selling of derivatives can be bewildering—even to economists—the basic concept is simple. In any agreement to buy or sell at a future date, both sides hope the price they agreed on will change in their favor, or at least stay the same.

SHORT SELLING

A trader in derivatives can make money even when the price falls, by what's called "short selling." For example, he can borrow (not buy) 100 shares, and sell them for $10 each, making $1,000. If the price drops to $5 per share, he buys them back for $500. He can then return the shares (plus a borrowing fee) to the lender, and keep the $500 difference.

See also: 74–75, 78–79

A **RISKY** business

MARKETS HAVE UPS AND DOWNS, AND PRICES RISE AND FALL WITH SUPPLY AND DEMAND. IT'S IMPOSSIBLE TO BE CERTAIN ABOUT WHAT WILL HAPPEN IN THE FUTURE. BUT TRADERS IN THE MARKETS HAVE TO MAKE DECISIONS ABOUT WHAT TO BUY AND SELL, BASED ON THEIR FORECASTS, AND TO SOME EXTENT CHOOSE HOW MUCH RISK THEY WANT TO TAKE.

What will tomorrow bring?

Just like every other aspect of life, all economic activity involves uncertainty and risk. If you buy tickets for a music festival, for example, you may have to book them months in advance, and you cannot be certain that the band you want to see will be performing, and there is a risk that the weather may be so bad that the festival is canceled. Businesses have to make similar decisions when they are planning for the future. In economics, there is a difference between risk and uncertainty. There are some things that can't be predicted, especially when we look a long way into the future, such as what kinds of technological advances will be made five years from now, or a disease may appear that completely destroys this year's coffee crop. The future is uncertain, and we can't know how that uncertainty will affect decisions we make today.

In everyday language, risk means the possibility of something bad happening, but to economists it can be a good or a bad thing.

Low risk, high risk

But there are things we can predict with some confidence, especially in the near future. For example, if a café has some regular customers, and the numbers have steadily increased, they will probably keep increasing for the foreseeable future. And a company making winter clothes knows that sales every year have started to pick up at the end of the summer, so they are likely to increase again this year. The risk of something different happening in both cases is low. But a business's plans may involve a high level of risk. A company may decide, for example, on the high-risk idea of producing a range of raincoats in the spring, despite forecasts of a warm, dry summer. If the weather turns out to be as predicted, the company will have lost money it could have made selling swimwear, but if it turns out to be wet all summer, they will be the only suppliers of suitable clothes and will make much more money. So, when businesses are planning to launch

BULL AND BEAR MARKETS

In the stock and bond markets, someone who forecasts that prices are going to go up is sometimes described as a "bull." The opposite of this—someone who predicts that prices will fall—is known as a "bear." So, a bull market is one in which prices are steadily rising, and a bear market is one in which prices are falling.

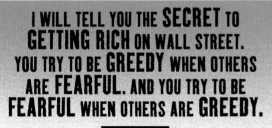

> **I WILL TELL YOU THE SECRET TO GETTING RICH ON WALL STREET. YOU TRY TO BE GREEDY WHEN OTHERS ARE FEARFUL. AND YOU TRY TO BE FEARFUL WHEN OTHERS ARE GREEDY.**
>
> **WARREN BUFFETT**

a product, or to buy supplies for the next season, they look at trends in the market to assess how much risk they are taking. Similarly, investors in businesses will also examine a company's record, whether its sales have been increasing, and prices rising, in order to see whether to buy shares in it or not.

See also: 86–87, 142–143

Feeling confident

For traders in any market, information about the past is a crucial tool in forecasting the future. It's a guide to gauging how much risk is involved in making decisions about buying and selling. There are many factors that affect future trends in the market, so calculating the degree of risk can be complex. It may even involve mathematical formulas and computer modeling. But the most sophisticated methods can't take into account every possibility, and their predictions can't be totally relied on. Often, economic decisions are based as much on hunches as complicated math. Experienced traders develop a "feel" for the market they work in, and rely on how confident they are about a business from past experience and how other traders are behaving. On the stock exchange the price of shares in a company depends as much on the confidence people have in the company as its actual performance.

⊙ What are the chances?
Although we can't predict the outcome of our economic decisions, we can calculate the probabilities. The least probable outcomes offer the greatest rewards.

THE HIGHER THE RISK, THE GREATER THE RETURN

See also: 50–51

An informed

THE WORLD OF FINANCIAL MARKETS, WHERE FINANCIAL PRODUCTS CALLED "SECURITIES" ARE TRADED, IS LIKE A CASINO. BUYERS AND SELLERS GAMBLE ON THEIR FUTURE VALUE. SOME BETS ARE SAFE, AND OTHERS RISKY. TRADERS HAVE SOPHISTICATED WAYS OF WORKING OUT THE ODDS OF MAKING MONEY, AND WAYS THEY HOPE TO MINIMIZE RISK.

What are financial products?

Like any other market, the activities of financial markets involve transactions between buyers and sellers. But it's the nature of the financial products that are traded that can make them hard to understand. To start with, they're not goods that can be seen or touched, but intangible things such as shares in a company, or bonds issued by governments. Also, buyers receive only a document as their proof of ownership for whatever they have bought, such as a bond or share certificate. These documents are what are known as financial instruments, and they represent the agreement between buyer and seller.

> The term "Minsky moment" was first used to describe the beginning of the Russian financial crisis in 1998.

Safe and secure?

Generally speaking, there are three different types of financial products or "securities" that are publicly traded. Some are in the form of company shares. Companies sell shares through the stock markets to raise money. A person buying these effectively owns part of that company, and the value of this shareholding, also known as equity, depends on how much profit the company makes. There are also "debt securities," which include bonds issued by corporations and governments. The buyer of these is in effect lending money to the issuer, rather than buying a share in the business, and the bond is a guarantee that the loan will be repaid at a certain date, plus an agreed to amount of interest. More complex financial instruments, such as forward contracts and other derivatives (see pp. 78–79) are also traded in the financial markets.

What's the risk?

Of course, the value of these securities can go up or down, like any other product traded in a market. Some, such as shares in a large and well-established company, or government bonds, are likely to be safe bets, bringing their owners a reasonable return on their

MINSKY MOMENT

US economist Hyman Minsky argued that periods of economic stability lead to overconfidence, with traders taking bigger risks in the belief that prices will keep on rising. Inevitably a time comes, the "Minsky moment," when confidence in these investments proves unfounded, borrowers can't repay their debts, and there is a financial crisis.

GAMBLE

money. But—and this is the gamble—buying more risky securities could bring a better profit. Advances in information technology have allowed traders in the financial markets to find new ways of calculating the risk of buying securities. They have employed financial analysts with training in math or physics rather than economics. Their aim has been to beat the system and find risk-free ways of making a profit. The analysts have created new financial products, such as derivatives of debt securities. These might include banks making loans to companies with no established reputation, or to individuals whose jobs may be at risk. Because the borrower may not pay back the loan it's a risky asset for the bank. But if they put some of these loans together with safer ones, they can sell them in a "package" as a debt security.

❷ Spreading the bets
The high risk of some investments can be hidden if they are included in a package of safer options, such as government bonds.

Traders can make even more complex financial products by bundling several packages together and selling parts of them.

Hidden danger
This "financial engineering" can appear almost risk-free, because unless a substantial number of debts aren't repaid the gamble should pay off. Unfortunately, the traders, who often don't have the mathematical abilities of the analysts, tend to become overconfident and underestimate the risks—just as a gambler gets reckless after a winning streak. And lenders, encouraged by how easily they can sell on the debts, offer ever more risky loans.

See also: 90–91, 126–127

TRADING IN FINANCIAL PRODUCTS IS A GAMBLE ON THEIR FUTURE VALUE

SHARES

LOANS

BONDS

SECURITIES

HYPERINFLATION

A CRISIS, SUCH AS A WAR, CAN SOMETIMES SET OFF A SPIRAL OF HYPERINFLATION IN A COUNTRY, WHEN PRICES SOAR BY HUNDREDS OR THOUSANDS OF PERCENT A YEAR. THE CURRENCY SOON BECOMES WORTHLESS AS PEOPLE RUSH TO SPEND MONEY BEFORE IT LOSES ITS VALUE. HYPERINFLATION IS OFTEN TRIGGERED BY THE GOVERNMENT PRINTING MONEY TO MAKE UP FOR A SHORTFALL IN INCOME OR RESERVES.

WEIMAR DISASTER

From 1921–24, the Weimar Republic (now Germany) suffered catastrophic hyperinflation. After paying vast amounts of gold in war damages, the Weimar government began printing money on a huge scale to maintain public spending. As a result, the value of the currency (the mark) fell and prices escalated wildly. In 1923, inflation hit 30,000 percent per month, with prices doubling every other day.

> "**Inflation** is as violent as a mugger, as frightening as an armed robber and as **deadly** as a **hit man**."
>
> RONALD REAGAN, US PRESIDENT 1981–1989

BIG BANKNOTES

000,000,000,000,000

Hyperinflation means prices rise astronomically and governments struggle to keep pace by printing banknotes of ever larger values. In Weimar Germany in 1922, the highest value note was 50,000 marks; the next year it was 100 trillion. Low denomination notes were so worthless that it was cheaper to paper your rooms in banknotes than buy wallpaper!

In 2015, you needed 35 quadrillion Zimbabwe dollars to buy one US dollar!

Wheelbarrow of money

Following a period of upheaval and uncertainty, the government may print more money in an attempt to kick-start spending. Unfortunately, this can lead to hyperinflation and skyrocketing prices that increase at an alarming rate.

THE VICTIMS

The hardest hit by hyperinflation are the less well-off. The rich survive by buying foreign currency, and in Weimar Germany, workers with unions were able to press for higher wages to keep up with prices. But the rest—such as farm and office workers—saw their wages lagging far behind soaring prices. For those living off savings and pensions, the plunge in what their money could buy was catastrophic.

4,000,000
6,000,000
12,000,000

50,000,000

ZIMBABWE

For a decade from the late 1990s, Zimbabwe suffered perhaps the worst period of hyperinflation ever. It began shortly after private farms were confiscated and the government began printing money to counter the fall off in production. Very quickly, prices in stores were changing several times a day and notes became so devalued that people resorted to taking their money to market in wheelbarrows. In November 2008 inflation peaked at an amazing 79.6 billion percent.

Is greed GOOD?

WHEN DESCRIBING HOW MARKETS WORK, THE ECONOMIST ADAM SMITH STATED THAT "IT IS NOT FROM THE BENEVOLENCE OF THE BUTCHER, THE BREWER OR THE BAKER THAT WE EXPECT OUR DINNER, BUT FROM THEIR REGARD TO THEIR OWN INTEREST." SO, IF EVERYBODY ACTS IN THEIR OWN INTEREST, WE CAN ALL BENEFIT. BUT IS IT REALLY ALL RIGHT TO BE SELFISH?

> THE PROBLEM OF **SOCIAL ORGANIZATION** IS HOW TO SET UP AN ARRANGEMENT UNDER WHICH **GREED** WILL DO THE **LEAST HARM**, **CAPITALISM** IS THAT KIND OF A SYSTEM.
>
> **MILTON FRIEDMAN**

It's all about me

When we're deciding what goods and services we're going to buy, and the price we're prepared to pay, we try to get the best deal we can for ourselves. It would be foolish not to. And the producers aren't providing those goods and services just for our benefit, but in order to make a profit, and they'll also try to get the best price they can. Everyone in the market is acting in his own interest. The result, argue economists who believe in free markets, is that everyone benefits. The producers sell their goods and make a profit, and the buyers pay a fair price for the things that they need and want. Competition with others in the market who are protecting their own interests spurs productivity and innovation, giving us new and better products and lower prices. Self-interest, the economists argue, is therefore a good thing.

A bigger share

But most people don't have such a rosy view of the way markets operate. Rather than just looking after their own interests, many businesses are seen as greedy and aggressive. Not happy with having enough to satisfy their needs, people are easily tempted to try to get more, without considering the needs and wants of others. Greedy businesses and consumers try to take more than their fair share, becoming rich at someone else's expense. Perhaps this unfairness is inevitable in a free market. It encourages people to act in their own interest and compete with one another to get the best possible deal for

See also: 46–47, 54–55

IS IT WRONG TO BE SELFISH... OR DOES EVERYONE BENEFIT IN THE END?

themselves. To an extent, the most selfish business will be the most successful. Greed, it would seem, is good for business.

We can't be sure

But it may not be so good for society as a whole. Aside from the morality of greed, whether it's right or wrong, it has some negative effects on the economy. Greedy businesses can get rich and powerful, forcing out their competitors and forming monopolies, which dominate the market. Consumers may lose out if producers prioritize profits above the quality of their products. And companies can fail if their managers take unnecessary risks to make quick profits. Also, if some people are making money at the expense of others, it's not only morally questionable, but also creates greater

> **WE HAVE ALWAYS KNOWN THAT HEEDLESS SELF INTEREST, WAS BAD MORALS, WE NOW KNOW IT IS BAD ECONOMICS.**
> FRANKLIN D ROOSEVELT, FORMER US PRESIDENT

Gordon Gekko, a lead character in the film *Wall Street*, claims "Greed... is good. Greed is right, greed works."

inequality, which in the long term is bad for the economy. The greatest problem though is that self-interest can encourage businesses to produce goods and services that damage the environment, with dire consequences for us all. For these reasons, governments often regulate businesses and markets to ensure that they're conducted in the interests of consumers and society as a whole, not only in the interests of businesses. Many socialist economists believe that competitive markets themselves are the problem, and greed just a symptom. Karl Marx stated that they should be abandoned and replaced with industries owned and run by the people. Others have been less extreme, advocating cooperative businesses that are owned and run by their members, the workers and consumers of that business, for their mutual benefit.

◔ Saint or sinner?

A rich businessman could be considered selfish, but it's possible for him to produce valuable goods or services and offer well-paid jobs, and still be successful.

INSIDER TRADING

In the stock market, a trader may gain private information about a company that will affect the price of that company's shares but that his customers don't know about. He could sell shares before their value goes down, or buy shares if he knows the value is going to go up. However, this kind of "insider trading" is illegal in many countries.

See also: 80–81, 82–83

Making the

MANY THEORIES IN ECONOMICS ARE BASED ON HOW THINGS WOULD WORK IN AN IDEAL WORLD, RATHER THAN HOW THEY WORK IN PRACTICE. BUT THE NEW FIELD OF BEHAVIORAL ECONOMICS STUDIES THE WAY THAT ECONOMIC DECISIONS ARE MADE IN THE REAL WORLD. IN FACT, IT EXAMINES HUMAN BEHAVIOR AS MUCH AS ECONOMICS.

"MY HUNCH IS IT SHOULD DO WELL"

"LOOKS LIKE A GOOD INVESTMENT"

"I CAN'T SEE IT FAILING"

"I'VE GOT A GOOD GUT FEELING ABOUT THIS"

MANY ECONOMIC THEORIES MAKE THE ASSUMPTION THAT DECISIONS ARE MADE RATIONALLY...

"SHOULD BE OK"

"THE LAST ONE DID WELL"

"SOMEBODY TOLD ME IT'S HIGHLY RECOMMENDED"

Economic man

One of the assumptions that is often made by economic theories is that people making economic decisions think rationally about them, and weigh up all the pros and cons. The theories are based on a sort of ideal "economic man" who represents the way that we all act when deciding whether to buy or sell something, or to save or invest our money. This ideal economic man also has access to all the necessary information, which he can use to come to a decision logically. But, of course, this ideal person doesn't exist and real people don't behave in a purely rational and calculating way. Rather than tell us that we ought to make decisions in a certain way, some economists have tried to find out how we actually do make them.

Just good enough

A pioneer of this field of behavioral economics was US political scientist Herbert Simon. He introduced ideas from psychology, sociology, and computer science to his study of economics in the later half of the 20th century. Simon noticed that when faced with an economic problem or choice, people don't always make the decision in a logical way, taking into account all the possibilities. It's not that we don't behave rationally, but that we have what Simon called "bounded rationality." One of the problems, he suggested, is that there's often too much to think about—economic problems involve many variables. And ordinary humans don't have minds like computers to

DANIEL KAHNEMAN (1934–)

A psychologist rather than an economist, Daniel Kahneman was joint winner of the Nobel Prize in Economic Sciences in 2002 for his work on decision-making. He was born in Tel Aviv, but grew up in Paris. In 1948, in the new State of Israel, he studied psychology, and went on to work in universities in Israel and the US with his long-time colleague Amos Tversky.

RIGHT decision

> **AFTER SEEING A LONG RUN OF RED ON THE ROULETTE WHEEL, MOST PEOPLE WRONGLY BELIEVE THAT BLACK IS NOW DUE.**
> **DANIEL KAHNEMAN & AMOS TVERSKY**

Make up your mind ⊙
When faced with making a decision, we generally act using intuition rather than rational thinking, because it's quicker and easier, and often gives us the result we want.

process all that information in a logical way. Instead, we use some general rules of thumb, or "heuristics." Although not an ideal solution, this allows us to make decisions that are "good enough."

Get real

Simon's work showed the links between economics and psychology, and two psychologists, Daniel Kahneman and Amos Tversky, developed the ideas further. Their studies were originally about decision-making in general, but are particularly relevant to the way we make economic decisions. Like Simon, they found that we tend to base our decisions on incomplete information, such as our personal experience or something we've heard about, rather than examining all the options. Because we want to make decisions quickly without thinking too deeply, we often make false assumptions or act on intuition, hunches, or what we would like to be the case. And sometimes, our thinking is just wrong. An example is the "gambler's fallacy": if you toss a coin and it comes up tails 10 times in a row, many people think that it's more likely to be heads next time, but in fact the odds are still 50:50

... BUT WE SELDOM TAKE INTO ACCOUNT THE TRUE PROBABILITIES INVOLVED.

> Given a choice of three similar items at different prices, we tend to choose the middle-priced one, not the cheapest.

no matter what's happened in the past. And with a little thought, we would know that this is true. Kahneman explains that we can think rationally, but it's quicker and easier to make decisions intuitively or emotionally. From this research into behavioral economics, economists are coming to realize that theories based on the perfectly rational behavior of "economic man" and the calculations and computer modeling of economic analysts may not give an entirely true picture of how economies work in the real world.

See also: 132–133, 142–143

FINANCIAL CRISIS OF 2007-8

IN SEPTEMBER 2008, TO EVERYONE'S SHOCK, THE GIANT INVESTMENT BANK LEHMAN BROTHERS FAILED. THE COLLAPSE MARKED THE BEGINNING OF WHAT MANY ECONOMISTS CONSIDER THE WORST FINANCIAL CRISIS SINCE THE GREAT DEPRESSION OF THE 1930S. MANY OTHER BANKS WERE SAVED FROM FAILURE ONLY BY BIG GOVERNMENT BAILOUTS. MANY PEOPLE LOST THEIR HOMES AND JOBS AND FOR A YEAR MARKETS AROUND THE WORLD STALLED.

ROOTS OF THE CRISIS

Few economists agree on the causes of the crisis. But one trigger was a failure of "subprime mortgages" in the US. These were mortgages lent to borrowers with poor credit histories. Bundles of these mortgages were passed on to financial "engineers" at the big banks who pooled them together to fund loans between banks. The problem was that when just a few borrowers were unable to make their mortgage payments, these interbank loans collapsed like a house of cards.

PACKAGES OF DEBT

Many people believe that after the banks were deregulated (when various rules were relaxed) in the 1980s, they became carried away by "financial engineering." Banks set up elaborate and risky schemes to make money by buying and selling things such as securities on loans, and created complex chains of debt. In effect, they gambled vast sums of money without the reserves to absorb losses. In the wake of the crisis, many cases of financial malpractice emerged.

Banking crisis ❯

When several banks failed in 2007 and 2008, it sparked a financial crash around the world. Trillions of dollars were lost and governments forced to intervene to save other banks from collapse.

TOO BIG TO FAIL

Faced with the collapse of major banks, governments stepped in. If these big banks failed, millions of ordinary account holders could face financial ruin. The banks were deemed "too big to fail" without disastrous consequences. But the debts they had built up were massive. In the US alone, bailing out the banks cost $16.8 trillion—a third of the country's GDP (gross domestic product). Some believe that the banks should have been left to fail.

GREAT RECESSION

The financial crisis of 2007–8 led into the Great Recession, a period of stalled economic growth around the world. Not every country was equally affected, but the downturn led to a shrinkage of the world's GDP in 2009 for the first time since World War II. Worried about the growing national debt, many governments cut back spending with "austerity" policies. Some economists argue that this tactic can make things worse.

In October 2008, $90 billion was wiped off the value of UK companies as markets collapsed.

"What **we know** about the **global financial crisis** is that we **don't know** very much."

PAUL SAMUELSON, WINNER OF THE 1970 NOBEL MEMORIAL PRIZE IN ECONOMIC SCIENCE

See also: 34–35, 76–77

Costing the

OVER THE PAST TWO CENTURIES, INDUSTRY HAS MADE MANY COUNTRIES
RICHER THAN EVER BEFORE. INDUSTRIALIZED COUNTRIES HAVE SEEN
CONTINUOUS ECONOMIC GROWTH AND IMPROVED LIVING STANDARDS.
BUT THIS PROSPERITY COMES AT A COST IN TERMS OF DAMAGE TO
OUR PLANET. AND IT'S A COST WE MUST START PAYING NOW.

Dire predictions

When the first modern industries were
established at the end of the 18th century
(see pp. 42–43), it seemed as if there were
no limits to the things they could produce.
There was an apparently infinite supply of
natural resources such as coal and iron
for the new industries, and even farms
became more productive with
increased mechanization.
As societies became richer,
they consumed more, and
industry satisfied the
demand by supplying more
goods. There was no reason
to believe that this continual
improvement in living
standards would ever end. Even
then, though, some economists had
doubts. Robert Malthus, for example,

The
population of the
world increased by
1 billion people, up to
7.3 billion, in the 12 years
from 2003 to 2015.

warned that populations were also
increasing, and that in time their rate
of consumption could outstrip supply.
Through the 19th and 20th centuries, his
warnings looked pessimistic, but in the
21st century world population has risen
drastically, increasing demand for essential
resources. It's also become clearer that
we live on a planet that has finite
resources, and that we'll have
to reduce our consumption of
them. There's a limit to the
amount of land that can be
used to produce food, for
example, and to the supply
of fresh water. But it's not only
food that we consume. Our
lifestyles have created a demand
for manufactured goods, energy, and
transportation that puts pressure on
supplies of resources such as coal, gas, oil,
and minerals that can never be replaced.

What's the damage?

Industrialization is also damaging the
environment. Obvious examples are the
smoky factories and diesel trucks that ruin
air quality in cities, but there are other
serious problems. Emissions of greenhouse
gases, like CO_2, cause global warming,
which is leading to changes to our climate
that threaten food production, and extreme
weather conditions and rising sea levels
that are destroying property and disrupting

COLLECTIVE ACTION

The problems of pollution, climate
change, and depletion of resources
are not limited to single countries,
and do not recognize national
borders. The solutions have to
be economic, but need political
will to enforce them. Measures
to reduce consumption and to
regulate industries must be adopted
globally, so it's vital that there is
international cooperation.

EARTH

THE KEY TO UNDERSTANDING THE FUTURE IS ONE WORD: SUSTAINABILITY.

PATRICK DIXON, BRITISH TRENDS FORCASTER

OUR PLANET'S FINITE NATURAL RESOURCES ARE DWINDLING AS OUR RATES OF CONSUMPTION ARE INCREASING.

businesses. Industry affects agricultural production in other ways, too. Pollution poisons our land, rivers, and seas, and farmland is used instead for manufacturing industries or extracting mineral resources. Attempts to increase agricultural production by clearing vast areas of rain forest, using herbicides and pesticides, and developing genetically modified crops, can upset the balance of ecosystems. The cost of industry's damage to the environment is already huge, and unless things change, it will put an end to the industrial era and its ever-increasing prosperity. It's as much an economic issue as a scientific one and it needs economic as well as scientific measures to solve it.

Punishing polluters

Economic measures could include making polluting companies pay more tax. Taxes on greenhouse gas emissions, or toxic waste, would push industries to find cleaner methods of production, while giving governments money to deal with the issues caused by pollution. Governments can also put caps, or limits, on emissions and punish industries that exceed their quotas, the amounts they're allowed to emit. In a system of emissions trading, non-polluting companies can sell their quota to other companies, so cleaner industries are rewarded, while polluting industries pay more.

⊕ A finite world

Earth has finite resources, and as our economies and populations grow, we consume more. Unless we learn to consume less, these resources will become scarcer and scarcer and ever more costly.

See also: 104–105, 112–113 →

FULL

EMPTY

PLAYING SAFE

When people invest in shares or other financial products, they aim to make a profit. But markets are constantly changing, so the value of their investment can go down as well as up. Some others may choose to make less profit and opt for a safer investment, such as government bonds or bank savings accounts.

RISE AND FALL

While many poor countries struggle to survive, others are developing fast with unprecedented economic growth, and some older developed countries are even in decline. Nothing in economics is certain, and it may be that in 100 years' time new economic powers will have replaced the US, Europe, and Japan.

Markets and trade
IN PRACTICE

ECONOMIC FORECASTS

Many economic decisions involve predicting what will happen in the future, such as whether prices will rise or fall. Economists today use complex computer modeling and algorithms to make forecasts, but even these can't take into account natural uncertainty, such as the weather, and the fact that people behave unpredictably.

SMUGGLING WEALTH

Most countries have some restrictions on what can and can't be imported. There may be taxes on certain goods, such as tobacco and alcohol, and others, such as guns and hard drugs, may be prohibited. But there's always a demand for these goods, and as a result smuggling them into the country can be very lucrative.

Global trade has made some countries rich, while poor countries also benefit from exporting goods. Demand for cheap goods has risen—along with foreign travel—so transportation is a major industry. This comes at an environmental cost, as air transportation, especially, emits large amounts of greenhouse gases that cause global warming.

COST OF TRANSPORTATION

A BASIC INCOME

Some economists, such as Milton Friedman, argue that the tax system should give money to people with low incomes. A "negative income tax" would replace welfare payments, ensuring that everybody has a guaranteed basic income. Anyone earning more would pay a proportion in income tax.

The countries of the developed world have grown rich through businesses trading in markets, and investment has helped economies grow. To help spread this wealth, governments make laws and impose taxes. But in the 21st century, businesses may face more restrictions in order to limit environmental damage.

CARBON FOOTPRINTS

Industrialization has brought prosperity, but each one of us is leaving a "carbon footprint"—the amount of carbon dioxide released into the atmosphere as a result of our actions. To limit the damage, some people think we must invent technology to deal with the pollution; others say we must stop using fossil fuels and find new energy sources.

PROTECTING PEOPLE

Some restrictions on free markets aren't made for purely economic reasons, but to protect people. As well as laws protecting consumers from harmful goods, there are laws in most countries on working conditions, in order to stop companies from exploiting workers in "sweatshops" where they receive low pay for long hours, or use child or slave labor.

Can money buy **HAPPINESS?**

Measuring a country's WEALTH

Who's providing the MONEY?

Making MONEY out of thin air

Why are some countries POOR?

The standard of living in many countries is higher than it has ever been. The wealth brought by modern industry and technology means that many people have more than they need, but at the same time, billions of people are living in poverty. One of the problems economists are dealing with is how to distribute the wealth more fairly, helping poorer countries to develop and encouraging economic growth.

Who benefits from GLOBALIZATION?

The POVERTY problem

Helping the DEVELOPING WORLD

PAYBACK time!

The WAGE gap

Measuring a country's **WEALTH**

THERE ARE NEARLY 200 COUNTRIES IN THE WORLD. SOME
COVER A LARGE AREA AND HAVE HUGE POPULATIONS,
WHILE OTHERS ARE SMALL AND SPARSELY POPULATED.
IN RICH COUNTRIES, SOME PEOPLE ENJOY A HIGH
STANDARD OF LIVING, BUT IN POOR COUNTRIES
A MAJORITY LIVE IN POVERTY. ECONOMISTS
TRY TO MEASURE THE INCOME OF COUNTRIES
TO SEE HOW RICH OR POOR THEY ARE.

Reaching a figure

There are many reasons why it's useful to
measure how rich a country is. We need to know
which countries are very poor and may need help
from richer countries. We also need to have an
idea of the standard of living in each country—
whether the people there have enough to live on.
It's helpful too if we can see whether a country is
becoming richer, or poorer, over time. It's fairly easy
to measure how rich a person is. We can see how much
money she has in the bank, what she owns, and most
importantly how much she earns. But measuring the wealth
of a whole country is not so simple, and economists have
suggested different ways of doing it. The generally accepted

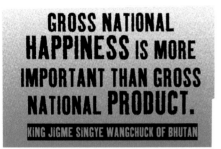

**GROSS NATIONAL
HAPPINESS IS MORE
IMPORTANT THAN GROSS
NATIONAL PRODUCT.**

KiNG JiGME SiNGYE WANGCHUCK OF BHUTAN

How rich is a country? ➋
The value of all the goods and
services produced in a country
gives us an idea of its income,
but how rich a country is
depends on things like the
size of its population.

measure is of the Gross Domestic Product (GDP) of the country. This is calculated by adding up the value of all the goods and services produced within the country in one year. These goods and services are bought and sold, so the GDP tells us about the economic activity in the country, and gives an idea of the country's income.

A false picture

But this may not give a true picture of how rich different countries are. Although the US has the largest GDP of all countries, there are others that are comparatively better off. A country like Luxembourg, for example, has a much smaller economy measured by GDP, but because its population is very small, people in Luxembourg are much richer on average than in the US. There are also countries that have a fairly large GDP, but are considered poor because of their huge populations.

A more accurate measure of how rich the people of a country are is GDP per capita—the total value of goods and services divided by the number of people in the country. GDP per capita is often used to give an idea of the standard of living of one country compared with another. But this too can be misleading, since it only shows us an average of how rich each inhabitant is. In many countries, the wealth is unevenly distributed, and most of the population may be living in poverty while a privileged few live in luxury. It's also tricky to compare the standard of living between countries because the cost of living may also be different. A person living comfortably in India, for example, would find it difficult to survive on the same income in Sweden, because things

are much more expensive there. GDP per capita is usually a measure of a country's economic activity over one year. Over time, these figures build up a picture of the economic growth of the country, whether it is becoming richer or poorer, and by how much.

See also: 104–105, 112–113

Paying out

GDP can tell us about countries' incomes, but to see how well a country is faring economically, we must also look at how much money is going out. Countries, like people, may borrow money for specific projects and have debts to repay. And most countries rely on some international trade, so it's important to note whether there's more money coming into the country than going out— this is described as a surplus—or more going out—this is a deficit.

> The countries with the biggest economies in the world are the USA, China, and Japan.

MEASURING HAPPINESS

It's often said that money can't buy you happiness. In 1972 the King of Bhutan stated that his country may be poor, but his people are happy, and argued there should be a measure of Gross National Happiness as well as GDP. Economists have taken the idea seriously and there is now an annual World Happiness Report, published by the United Nations.

TO COMPARE THE STANDARD OF LIVING OF DIFFERENT COUNTRIES, WE HAVE TO MEASURE THEIR WEALTH AND POPULATION.

Who's providing the **MONEY?**

BUSINESSES MAKE MONEY BY SELLING THEIR GOODS OR SERVICES. THIS INCOME IS USED TO PAY THE COSTS OF THINGS SUCH AS RAW MATERIALS, MACHINERY, AND WORKERS. BUT FIRMS ALSO NEED TO RAISE MONEY TO START A NEW BUSINESS OR TO BUY NEW MACHINES OR BUILDINGS, BEFORE THE MONEY FROM SALES STARTS COMING IN.

> IT'S NOT THE **EMPLOYER** WHO **PAYS** THE **WAGES.** EMPLOYERS ONLY HANDLE THE MONEY. IT'S THE **CUSTOMER** WHO PAYS THE **WAGES.**
>
> HENRY FORD, AMERICAN INDUSTRIALIST

See also: 48–49, 52–53

Raising funds

Almost every business, from big corporations down to small one-person companies, needs to raise money at some point, in addition to the income it receives from selling its goods or services. To get a business off the ground, for example, involves some start-up costs such as buying tools and machinery, renting or buying a building or vehicles for transporting goods, and hiring workers. Later, a business might want to expand, launch a new product, or update its computer system. All of these things cost money, which often has to be paid out before there is any income from sales.

There are a number of ways in which a business can raise the money it needs to operate. It can decide to borrow money, which it then pays back to the lender over a period of time. This arrangement means that the business has the money when it needs it, and pays it back when it makes money from sales. Alternatively, a larger business can become a public company and sell shares to investors. The advantage of this is that it is not a loan that the company will have to pay back. Instead, the shareholders' money buys them a part-ownership of the company, giving them a say in how the business is run, and a percentage of any future profits.

Who will pay?

Whichever way a business decides to raise money, through borrowing or selling shares, lenders and shareholders expect something in return for their money. The most usual source of loans for business are banks, which will lend money at an agreed to rate of interest (a percentage of the total loan) over a period of time. The bank makes an overall profit from

FRIEDRICH HAYEK (1899–1992)

A leading economist of the Austrian School, and joint winner of the Nobel Prize for economics in 1974, Hayek was born and studied in Vienna. He taught at the London School of Economics, before moving to the University of Chicago. Strongly anti-communist, Hayek developed free-market economic theories centered on privately financed businesses, free from government control.

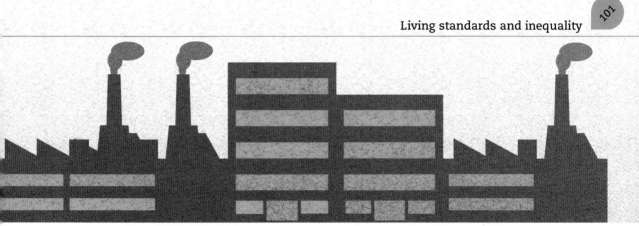

THERE ARE SEVERAL WAYS BUSINESSES CAN RAISE MONEY

MONEY BORROWED BY COMPANIES AS LOANS FROM BANKS; GIVEN AS GRANTS OR SUBSIDIES BY GOVERNMENT; PAYMENTS FOR SHARES FROM SHAREHOLDERS, BANKS, OTHER COMPANIES, OR GOVERNMENTS.

RETURNS TO LENDERS AS LOAN REPAYMENTS + INTEREST; OR PART OWNERSHIP OF THE COMPANY AND A SHARE OF THE PROFITS.

this, since the business has to pay back the original loan plus interest. But it's not only banks that lend money to businesses. Large companies can also sell corporate bonds, effectively borrowing money from private investors that will be paid back later. Governments also often offer loans to companies, particularly to help new businesses start up, or to encourage industries that will benefit the community. Some industries, such as producers of renewable energy, may even be given grants or subsidies by the government that don't have to be repaid.

> Borrowers often have to provide security, such as a building they own, which they may lose if they default.

Buying in

There are several different kinds of investors who choose to buy shares in companies. Some are private individuals, but a large proportion of shareholders are commercial concerns, such as investment companies, pension funds, and banks. Governments also buy shares in privately owned companies, not only as an investment to share in the profits, but also to have some control over the company—they may even buy the majority of the shares to bring the company into public ownership, for example, if they need to bail out a failing bank.

In addition to this public investment in commercial businesses, state-owned enterprises such as national health-care systems, prisons, railroads, or energy companies, may also offer a share of that business to private investors. This will raise money for the government to invest in these services in addition to the funds gleaned from taxes.

See also: 116–117, 134–135

Making **MONEY** out of thin air

BECAUSE MONEY IS USED TO PAY FOR THINGS, IT IS CONSTANTLY CHANGING HANDS AND CIRCULATING WITHIN AN ECONOMY. WORKERS GET PAID THEIR WAGES, WHICH THEY SPEND ON GOODS AND SERVICES, AND THAT MONEY IS USED TO PRODUCE MORE GOODS AND PAY MORE WAGES. THE SUPPLY OF MONEY DOESN'T COME FROM NOWHERE, IT IS CREATED BY BANKS.

New money

The amount of money in circulation in an economy, known as the money supply, isn't fixed, but responds to changes in the economy as a whole. Sometimes demand for money is greater than at other times, for example, when businesses are expanding and wanting to borrow more money. It's the job of the banks to supply the money, but it has to come from somewhere, it can't just be made from thin air.

Passing it on

In fact, banks do have a way of creating new money, by using the money that's already in circulation. A bank's business basically consists of two things: looking after the money that people deposit in it, and making loans to people who need money. The bank uses money that's deposited to lend to other customers. But this system also provides a way of adding to the supply of money in circulation. Customer A, for instance, has $100, which she deposits in the bank. The bank then lends $90 to B. A still has access to her $100, should she need it, but B has access to $90 of credit, too, making a total of $190 in the money supply. The bank, meanwhile has only $10 in reserve. Now, let's say B spends the $90, using it to pay C's wages, and C deposits it in the bank.

The bank can then use that money to give a loan to D... and so on. The bank is lending more money than it actually has, but so long as the borrowers pay the money back, and the depositors don't withdraw all their money at once, the bank can increase the money supply by several times more than it has in reserve.

Keeping control

Of course, the business of "creating" money like this has to be very carefully regulated, and there are laws about how much the banks can add to the money supply. In most countries, the banks are overseen by a central bank set up by the government, such as the Bank of England or the US Federal Reserve. The central bank controls the amount of money in circulation by deciding how much the banks can lend compared to their reserves, and the amount of interest they can charge. The central bank itself can lend money, for example, to a bank that needs

BERNIE MADOFF

After Ponzi's massive fraud (see below), most investors were suspicious of any investment that seemed too good to be true. But 60 years later, thousands of people were taken in by the biggest fraud the US has ever seen. Investment adviser Bernie Madoff was jailed in 2009 for running a Ponzi scheme for more than 25 years, costing his clients a total of about $18 billion.

to pay out more than it has in reserve. The central bank can also increase the money supply directly by printing more money—or adding it electronically—which it can lend to governments or corporations. Creating money in this way is known as "quantitative easing."

But if the banks can make money apparently from nowhere, then so can more unscrupulous dealers. Probably the most famous of these was the Italian businessman Charles Ponzi, who operated an illegal scheme during the 1920s in the US, offering investors fantastic profits. His system, now known as a "Ponzi scheme," was to pay the first investors with money he got from subsequent investors. Because the profits the early investors got were so high, he rapidly attracted more investors, and made millions of dollars before he was found out.

See also: 112–113, 124–125

In the 1920s, Charles Ponzi's investors lost a total of about $20 million, more than $200 million today.

BANKS CONTROL THE AMOUNT OF MONEY IN THE ECONOMY

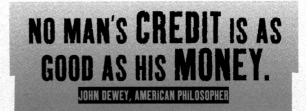

NO MAN'S **CREDIT** IS AS GOOD AS HIS **MONEY**.
JOHN DEWEY, AMERICAN PHILOSOPHER

◑ Creating money

Central banks control the money supply, that is the amount of money in the economy. They can decide to create more money to lend, which increases the amount in circulation.

Why are some countries **POOR?**

MANY COUNTRIES ARE RICHER THAN EVER BEFORE. THEIR INDUSTRIES ARE PRODUCTIVE AND THEIR ECONOMIES GROWING, SO PEOPLE IN THESE DEVELOPED COUNTRIES CAN HAVE LIFE'S NECESSITIES PLUS MANY LUXURIES. BUT THERE ARE OTHER COUNTRIES THAT HAVEN'T DEVELOPED IN THE SAME WAY AND HAVE A MUCH SMALLER SHARE OF THE WORLD'S WEALTH.

The 62 richest people in the world have as much wealth as the poorest 50% of the world's population—3.5 billion people.

> NO SOCIETY CAN SURELY BE FLOURISHING AND HAPPY, OF WHICH THE FAR GREATER PART OF THE MEMBERS ARE POOR AND MISERABLE.
> ADAM SMITH

We're all different

There are many natural differences between the countries of the world, such as their size and their climate, so it's not surprising that their economies are different, too. The countries that are richest in the modern world have become prosperous through economic development. That is, they have improved their industries to make them more efficient and productive, and adopted capitalist economic systems that have brought economic growth and encouraged advances in technology.

Getting rich

Countries in Europe, and later America and Japan, were the first to become industrialized, and began to enjoy a standard of living that was continually improving. This productivity gave them an advantage over less-developed countries, which found it difficult to compete for world trade. As a result, these poorer countries couldn't earn enough from their trade to build industries and

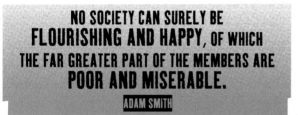

SOME COUNTRIES HAVE MORE THAN ENOUGH...

develop their economies. Some rich European countries built empires, colonizing countries around the world and exploiting them to get the resources they needed. So, while the rich countries grew richer, their colonies were unable to benefit from their own resources. But some underdeveloped countries have become rich, too. The nations of the Arabian Gulf, Saudi Arabia and Qatar, for example, consisted largely of a desert-dwelling population with no industry until oil was discovered in the region. Then they suddenly became among the richest countries in the world.

Held back

Many poor countries have struggled due to a lack of modern industry, leaving them unable to cash in on their resources. Many still have an agricultural economy, with small farms and fishing communities producing only enough food for local people, while larger agricultural businesses export their produce. Manufacturing industries tend to rely on cheap labor, and transporting goods is made difficult by bad roads and railroads. Some poorer countries are now being helped by investment from foreign countries and companies, and are called "developing countries."

NORTH AND SOUTH

If you look at a map showing the richest countries of the world, you will see that they are all in the northern hemisphere. The industrialization that made them economically successful spread fast across Europe and North America from Britain. However, many countries in Africa, South America, and Asia lagged behind, and their industries are still struggling to compete.

Many governments have adopted policies to encourage modern industries, making the most of their resources and promoting trade. Money from the new industries and investment from abroad is used to improve infrastructure such as communication, roads, and power lines. Developing countries are achieving unprecedented growth, but they face continued competition from developed countries. While conditions are improving for some, much of the world's population still lives in poverty.

Wealth and poverty ❷
People in rich, industrialized countries can enjoy a high standard of living with all modern conveniences, but in many parts of the world it's a struggle to survive.

See also: 108–109, 112–113

... OTHERS HAVE ONLY THE BARE NECESSITIES.

INTERNATIONAL FINANCIAL

SINCE WORLD WAR II, THE WORLD'S ECONOMIES AND MONEY SYSTEMS HAVE BECOME HIGHLY ENTANGLED. A WEB OF ORGANIZATIONS CALLED INTERNATIONAL FINANCIAL INSTITUTIONS (IFIs) OVERSEE THE FLOW OF MONEY BETWEEN NATIONS AND PROVIDE LOANS TO HELP COUNTRIES DEVELOP. THERE ARE MANY IFIs, INCLUDING THE INTERNATIONAL MONETARY FUND (IMF) AND THE WORLD BANK.

PEGGING CURRENCIES

000,000,000,000,000

In the Depression of the 1930s, many countries devalued their currencies to promote exports. This shrank the market and prolonged the slump. To stop this, world leaders met in 1944 and agreed to peg currencies against (maintain a set exchange rate with) the US dollar. They set up the International Monetary Fund (IMF) for emergency funding and the World Bank to lend money for long-term development.

TRADE AND LABOR

IFIs look after money flows between countries and are like banks. But nations are also linked by other organizations. The World Trade Organization (WTO), set up in 1994, oversees trade, and regulates 95 percent of the world's financial services. It has legal powers to enforce its rules. The International Labor Organization tries to ensure fair working conditions around the world but lacks legal power.

INSTITUTIONS

ⓥ Global bank

Several organizations, including the World Bank and International Monetary Fund, control financial transactions around the world. They lend funds to developing countries but these will have conditions attached.

In 2015, Ireland paid a billion euros in interest to the IMF for a bailout received in 2010.

WASHINGTON CONSENSUS

A loan from an IFI to a country in trouble comes with conditions. The IFIs impose measures, known as the Washington Consensus, to help the country's economy. Countries must, for instance, open up markets to international trade and reduce government intervention. But many argue the Consensus doesn't help the poorest people and simply increases the influence of global businesses.

> "The **world** is governed by **institutions** that are **not democratic**— the World Bank, the IMF, the WTO."

JOSE SARAMAGO, WINNER OF NOBEL PRIZE IN LITERATURE, 1998

GREEK BAILOUT

In 2009, Greece faced huge debts. The European Commission, European Central Bank, and IMF (the Troika or group of three) agreed to a bailout. In return the government had to make cuts in spending and sell state assets. In 2015, with services failing and unemployment rising, the Greek people voted in a new government in the hope of reversing the cuts. But the Troika bailout depended on the cuts continuing, so the country remains in turmoil.

Who benefits from

MODERN COMMUNICATIONS AND TRANSPORTATION MEAN GOODS CAN
BE TRADED TO AND FROM ANYWHERE IN THE WORLD. MULTINATIONAL
COMPANIES HAVE BROUGHT MODERN INDUSTRIES TO DEVELOPING
COUNTRIES, AND EVERY COUNTRY CAN TRADE IN THE GLOBAL MARKET.
EVERYONE SHOULD BENEFIT FROM THIS, YET MANY COUNTRIES DO NOT.

> Coca cola is sold
> in every country in
> the world, except
> North Korea.

See also: 104-105

Slow starters

Some countries benefit from globalization more
than others. Of course, globalization has opened
up a wide market, giving poorer countries a
huge number of potential customers for their
products. But unless they have a valuable
natural resource, such as oil or gold, which is
scarce elsewhere, they'll have to compete with
other countries to buy raw materials or to sell
manufactured products. The trouble is that in
the global marketplace, the poorer developing
countries start at a disadvantage
compared to the richer, industrialized countries. They
may be mainly agricultural or mining countries, with
little or no manufacturing industry. And because they
have no modern machinery, they can't exploit their
natural resources as efficiently and cheaply as
developed countries. To compete, they lower their
prices and make less profit. As a result, the workforce
is poorly paid, and there's little money to develop the
industries that would help their economies grow.

A helping hand

It's not that these countries have nothing to offer the
developed world. Some are rich in natural resources,
and all have human resources in the form of people
willing to work. But they haven't found ways to make
their businesses efficient and productive. This is
where companies in the developed world can help.
Multinational corporations can provide the machinery,
infrastructure, and technology that developing
countries need by setting up industries there, using
the natural resources available and employing local
labor. This arrangement benefits both the company
and the host country. The company gains easy access
to resources and cheap labor, and in return brings

DOING THE DIRTY WORK

As countries grow richer, polluting
industries become less acceptable,
and people less willing to do dirty
or dangerous work. Multinational
companies often move these
industries to developing countries,
where environmental and
employment regulations are
less strict. While this may have
short-term benefits for the local
economy, it may lead to long-
lasting and expensive damage.

GLOBALIZATION?

THE INTERNATIONAL COMMUNITY... ALLOWS NEARLY 3 BILLION PEOPLE—ALMOST HALF OF ALL HUMANITY—TO SUBSIST ON $2 OR LESS A DAY IN A WORLD OF UNPRECEDENTED WEALTH.

KOFI ANNAN, FORMER SECRETARY-GENERAL OF THE UNITED NATIONS

modern industry and investment to the local economy. In many places, foreign businesses have transformed poor rural communities into modern industrial towns, and people have been lifted out of poverty by the chance to earn regular wages.

The downside

Although foreign companies boost the local economy, and pay to improve roads, railroads, and airports, they own the industrial buildings and machinery. And while they employ local workers, these are often unskilled jobs, while the managers come from the company's home country. The bulk of the profits from the business go to the company, not the host country, and some multinationals pay little or no local tax. Nevertheless, while the company operates in a developing country, it brings a prosperity that that country often couldn't achieve on its own.

Critics of multinational companies argue that they don't establish local industries and promote sustainable growth. And it's the multinational, not the host country, that's trading in the global market, doing little to provide technology or give workers the skills to set up competitive local businesses. Furthermore, in the longer term, poor countries may come to rely on multinationals to achieve growth.

PROFITS GO BACK TO THE MULTINATIONAL, NOT TO THE HOST COUNTRY.

Give and take ➋
While globalized industry can provide jobs locally, the profits are often channeled straight back to the home country rather than benefitting the local economy.

The **POVERTY** problem

BILLIONS OF PEOPLE ALL AROUND THE WORLD ARE LIVING IN POVERTY. THEY DON'T HAVE ENOUGH MONEY TO BUY FOOD AND CLOTHES FOR THEMSELVES OR THEIR FAMILIES, AND THEY SURVIVE IN MISERABLE CONDITIONS WITHOUT ACCESS TO CLEAN WATER, HEATING, AND LIGHT. EVEN IN RICH COUNTRIES, THERE ARE SOME PEOPLE WHO ARE STRUGGLING TO SURVIVE.

> IN A COUNTRY **WELL GOVERNED,** POVERTY IS SOMETHING TO BE ASHAMED OF. IN A COUNTRY **BADLY GOVERNED, WEALTH** IS SOMETHING TO BE ASHAMED OF.
>
> **CONFUCIUS, CHINESE PHILOSOPHER**

More than one billion people do not have access to a toilet.

Unequal world

Modern industries and economic systems have brought prosperity to many parts of the world. Advances in technology have made these industries more productive, and careful management of economies has ensured that they continue to grow. Industrialized countries in the developed world have all the goods and services that they need, and more. What they can't produce for themselves, they can buy from elsewhere. In the richest countries, food and other goods are so plentiful that they go to waste. The world is producing more than it's ever done, yet almost half of its population doesn't have any of the comforts of modern life. There are many reasons for this appalling inequality, but the solutions to what has become an international poverty problem can be examined by economics.

How poor is poor?

It's important to understand what we mean when we talk about poverty. Rich and poor are relative terms, and someone who's considered poor in a country such as Norway, for example, would be seen as a rich person in somewhere like Burundi or the Central African Republic. But many international organizations, including the United Nations (UN) and the World Bank, believe there's such a thing as "absolute poverty"—having less than is necessary to live a proper life. A UN declaration lists the minimum basic human needs as food, clean water, sanitation, health care, shelter, education, and information. The declaration defines absolute poverty as being deprived of some or all of these necessities of life.

Another way of defining poverty is by measuring income. The World Bank, for instance, has suggested an international "poverty line," set at around $2 per day. Anyone earning below that level of income can be described as living in poverty. But because the cost of living can vary greatly from country to country, this definition doesn't accurately indicate all levels of poverty. Perhaps a better way would be to measure not what people have, but what they don't have—the things that they're deprived of.

BORROWING TO...

... REPAY DEBTS...

BUT SPENDING MORE...

ON DEBT REPAYMENTS...
LEADS TO MORE...

... DEBT

It's all relative

This level of absolute poverty is seldom found in countries in the developed world. But of course there are people who are relatively poor in even the richest countries. This kind of relative poverty (as opposed to absolute poverty) is when people cannot afford the things that are normal for the community they live in, and their standard of living is below what that society expects as a basic minimum. In these richer countries, the problems of relative poverty can be tackled by governments, by providing welfare payments to the sick and the unemployed, for example, and pensions for older people. They can also offer financial benefits to low-paid workers, and introduce laws to ensure employers pay a minimum wage.

In poorer countries, governments don't have the resources to provide for those living in poverty. They may also be caught in a "poverty trap," borrowing money to deal with their immediate problems, and not having anything left to develop their economies. So, they not only remain poor, but now have the additional burden of paying back the debt.

See also: 104–105, 112–113

⬆ The debt spiral

Often people find it impossible to get out of poverty. They borrow money, but don't earn enough money to pay the debt back. They then borrow more money, and end up with debts that can never be repaid.

JOHN MAYNARD KEYNES (1883–1946)

Born in Cambridge, England, Keynes changed economists' view of the world with his pioneering macroeconomics. He was an economic adviser at the Peace Conference after World War I, and to the British government. During the Great Depression in the 1930s, he explained how governments could use taxes and regulations to lessen the effects of economic ups and downs, and avoid financial crises.

Helping the DEVELOPING WORLD

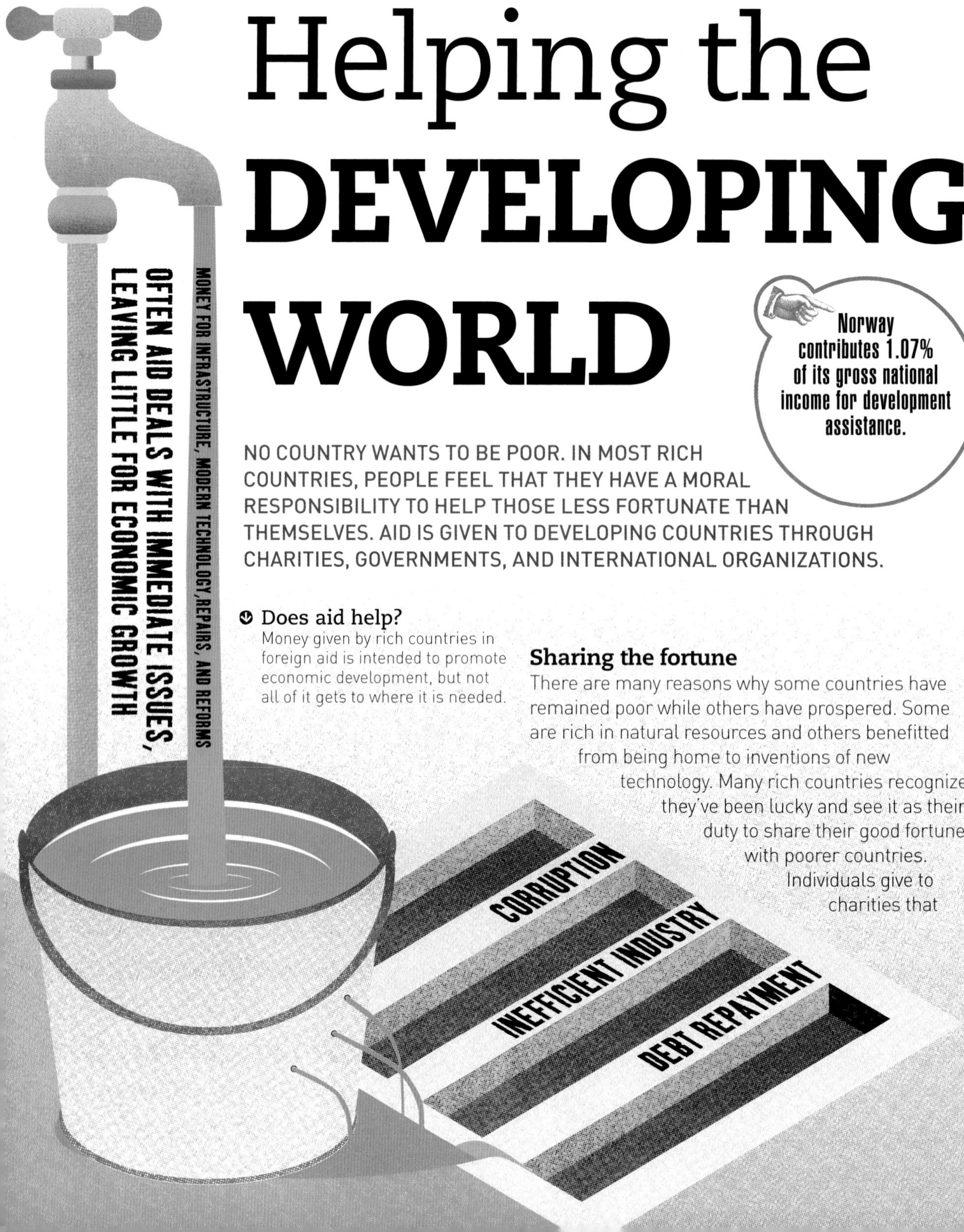

OFTEN AID DEALS WITH IMMEDIATE ISSUES, LEAVING LITTLE FOR ECONOMIC GROWTH

MONEY FOR INFRASTRUCTURE, MODERN TECHNOLOGY, REPAIRS, AND REFORMS

Norway contributes 1.07% of its gross national income for development assistance.

NO COUNTRY WANTS TO BE POOR. IN MOST RICH COUNTRIES, PEOPLE FEEL THAT THEY HAVE A MORAL RESPONSIBILITY TO HELP THOSE LESS FORTUNATE THAN THEMSELVES. AID IS GIVEN TO DEVELOPING COUNTRIES THROUGH CHARITIES, GOVERNMENTS, AND INTERNATIONAL ORGANIZATIONS.

Does aid help?

Money given by rich countries in foreign aid is intended to promote economic development, but not all of it gets to where it is needed.

Sharing the fortune

There are many reasons why some countries have remained poor while others have prospered. Some are rich in natural resources and others benefitted from being home to inventions of new technology. Many rich countries recognize they've been lucky and see it as their duty to share their good fortune with poorer countries. Individuals give to charities that

CORRUPTION

INEFFICIENT INDUSTRY

DEBT REPAYMENT

provide food and clean water to the poor. Governments in the developed world often set aside a percentage of the money from taxpayers to provide foreign aid, and together support international institutions like the World Bank, which provides financial help for projects in developing countries. Many businesses donate to charity or invest in industry overseas.

Not getting through

But not everyone agrees with giving foreign aid like this. There are some who argue, wrongly, that countries are poor because the people are lazy or corrupt, and they don't deserve to be helped. Others point out that often the money we give isn't being

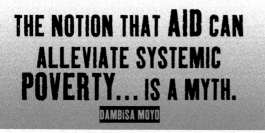

THE NOTION THAT **AID** CAN ALLEVIATE SYSTEMIC POVERTY... IS A MYTH.
DAMBISA MOYO

used in the right way. It isn't reaching the people who need it most, and isn't helping poor countries to develop and become prosperous. Even people within poor countries realize that money alone isn't enough to tackle the causes of poverty. Much of the money from charities, for example, is spent in providing things like food and clothing, or medicines and doctors, to people living in poverty. While this deals with their immediate needs, it doesn't provide for the future.

Foreign aid is sometimes given to the governments of poor countries, but does not reach the people who need it. This can be because they live in remote areas and do not have access to transportation, or because the government manages the money badly or uses it for its own projects rather than to help its citizens. Some poor countries have borrowed money from organizations such as the World Bank, but this hasn't been enough to establish a stable and growing economy, and they have ended up with the long-term burden of repaying that debt.

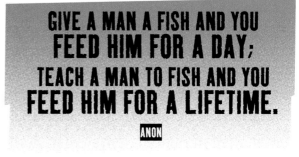

GIVE A MAN A FISH AND YOU **FEED HIM FOR A DAY;** TEACH A MAN TO FISH AND YOU **FEED HIM FOR A LIFETIME.**
ANON

Grow your own

A longer-term solution is to help poor countries develop their economies. Unless they can set up efficient industries and productive businesses to provide for themselves, they'll always be reliant on foreign aid. Rich countries can help by providing money for specific projects, such as improving the infrastructure—transportation links and communications—providing education and skills training, and helping to set up modern industries and small businesses. At the same time, they can support governments that encourage the building of a sound economy, tackling bad practices like corruption and tax evasion. When the country is economically independent, it will be able to trade with richer countries in the global market.

See also: 104–105, 106–107

A FRESH START

A number of the very poorest countries in the world are caught in a "poverty trap," having to spend more than they earn to repay money they have borrowed. Rather than being given more money, which would immediately disappear in debt repayments, these countries are asking to be given a fresh start by simply canceling their debts.

PROVIDING ENERGY

ENERGY IS VITAL TO EVERY ECONOMY. BUT RESOURCES ARE IN SHORT SUPPLY IN SOME COUNTRIES, AND RESERVES OF SOME FUELS WILL EVENTUALLY RUN OUT. ENERGY USE IS CHANGING OUR CLIMATE AS BURNING FOSSIL FUELS PUMPS GREENHOUSE GASES INTO OUR ATMOSPHERE, CAUSING GLOBAL WARMING.

ENERGY SECURITY

Modern economies need secure access to cheap energy. Relying on imported oil leaves economies vulnerable to foreign wars and social unrest. They must also compete for energy supplies with expanding economies such as China. In the short-term, they may have to deal with unpleasant regimes, or even go to war to protect supply lines. However, in the long term, some economies look to build security by finding new energy sources at home, such as nuclear power, or developing renewable sources.

FOSSIL FUELS

Fossil fuels—coal, oil, and natural gas—are made from buried remains of living things. They provide over 80 percent of our energy needs. Many of these fuel reserves are in politically unstable places such as the Middle East, so some countries are developing sources, including oil tar sands and oil shale, from which it is harder to extract oil but which are closer to hand. Even so, the world may run out of oil within the next half century.

⊙ Keeping the lights on

Establishing secure sources of energy is a preoccupation of many countries around the world. At the same time, alternative sources of energy need to be found before fossil fuels run out.

RENEWABLE AND SUSTAINBLE

"Renewable" sources of energy are those that never run out or are continually renewed. But the link between burning fossil fuels and global warming creates an urgent need to develop energy sources that are also "sustainable," meaning they can be used long term with no damaging effects. Key renewable and sustainable sources are water, wind, and solar power.

> "We need to find a new, **sustainable path** to the future we want. We need a **clean** industrial revolution."
>
> **BAN Ki-MOON**

REDUCING CONSUMPTION

Burning fossil fuels damages our planet, so many experts argue that we must also reduce consumption. At the international climate change conference in Paris in 2015, the countries of the world committed to keep global temperature rises "well below 3.5°F (2°C)," largely by cutting consumption of fossil fuels. Many developed countries have pledged to cut carbon emissions by the energy sector in half.

Energy use has tripled over the last 50 years—most of the increase is in fossil fuels.

PAYBACK time!

See also: 106–107, 108–109

THE MAIN JOB OF BANKS IS TO LEND MONEY. THEY ENABLE PEOPLE, BUSINESSES, AND EVEN COUNTRIES TO PAY FOR THE THINGS THEY NEED BUT DON'T HAVE ENOUGH MONEY FOR. BUT BANKS ARE BUSINESSES, TOO, AND EXPECT TO MAKE A PROFIT. SO BORROWERS HAVE TO PAY BACK MORE THAN THEY ORIGINALLY BORROWED—THEIR LOAN PLUS INTEREST.

The business of borrowing

Almost everybody borrows money at some time. It can be a very small amount, such as when you forget your wallet and borrow $3 from a friend to buy a cup of coffee. Of course, you promise to pay it back, perhaps the next day. Because you know and trust each other, your friend knows she will get her money back. If it's a larger amount, somebody wanting to borrow money goes to a bank. The bank will want to make sure that it will get its money back, so it will want to know about the borrower. If it's an individual, the bank asks about her job and income, for example. And if it's a business, the bank finds out how well the firm has been doing and what plans it has for the future. If the bank is sure that the borrower will be able to repay the money, they can make an agreement setting out the terms of the loan, such as when it will be paid back and whether it will be paid in installments or all at once. Unlike when you lend a few dollars to a friend, a bank isn't doing this out of kindness, but to make a profit. Normally it charges interest on the loan, adding a percentage known as the "interest rate" to the original amount borrowed.

A bank may agree to lend a business say $10,000 over a period of five years at an interest rate of 10% per annum (each year), which the business repays in monthly installments. Interest is charged on the money that's still owed, the bank gets back more than it loaned, but the borrower benefits from having a lump sum and time to pay it back.

> Lenders calculate their interest rates from a base rate, which is usually set by the central bank.

Feeling secure

Sometimes things can go wrong. A borrower may lose his job, or a business may fail to sell its goods, and they can't pay back the money they've borrowed. If the borrower defaults, that is, he doesn't make repayments as promised in the loan

GREEK DEBT CRISIS

After the global financial crisis in 2008, the Greek government was struggling to repay the money that it had borrowed. Other European countries, with the International Monetary Fund (IMF), arranged a "rescue package" of billions of euros to bail out the Greek economy, but this wasn't enough to prevent Greece, in 2015, from becoming the first country to default on an IMF loan.

> ## IF YOU OWE YOUR BANK A **HUNDRED POUNDS**, YOU HAVE **A PROBLEM. BUT IF YOU OWE A MILLION**, IT HAS.
> **JOHN MAYNARD KEYNES**

TO BUY A HOUSE MOST PEOPLE NEED A MORTGAGE,

A high price to pay
A person may take out a large loan, or mortgage, to buy a house. The bank works out a repayment plan based on his earnings. If the repayments aren't made the house must be sold to pay back the bank.

WHICH IS A LOAN THAT THEY MUST PAY BACK...

PLUS INTEREST

MONTHLY SALARY	MORTGAGE PAYMENT

SOLD $$$$$$

agreement, the bank loses money. To protect themselves against default, before giving a large loan, banks ask the borrower to provide security, such as a house, to back up the loan. If the borrower defaults, the bank can take the house to cover its loss. Most loans from a bank are secured loans, to protect the lender in case of default. If a borrower can't offer any security, the bank may still agree to lend money, but will charge a much higher rate of interest, because of the greater risk involved. Lenders can, in fact, make more profit by taking higher risks, such as on unsecured loans, or loans to individuals or companies who can't prove that they'll be able to continue making their repayments.

Footing the bill
Sometimes, banks make bad decisions, and gambles on risky loans don't pay off. Some have lost money. But in addition to lending money, they are looking after money that's been deposited with them, and the depositors would suffer if the bank went bust. To stop this, a central bank may step in to bail out a failing bank using public money. This may seem unfair because the bank can make a lot of money if things go well, but doesn't have to pay if things go wrong. This is called "moral hazard," which US economist Paul Krugman describes as when "one person makes the decision about how much risk to take, while someone else bears the cost if things go badly."

See also: 134–135

The **WAGE** gap

See also: 56-57, 64-65

The top 10% of earners in the US make more than half of the country's total income.

THE FREE MARKET SYSTEM THAT DEVELOPED OVER CENTURIES HAS PROVED TO BE AN EFFICIENT WAY TO MATCH SUPPLY AND DEMAND OF GOODS AND SERVICES. BUT NOT EVERYBODY BENEFITS FROM IT TO THE SAME EXTENT. COMPETITION IS AN ESSENTIAL ELEMENT OF A FREE MARKET, AND THERE ARE BOTH WINNERS AND LOSERS.

Free but not equal

With increasing globalization of trade and industry, we often compare the wealth of different countries, and their standard of living, using statistics such as GDP per capita (see pp. 98-99). But what these figures don't tell us, is how that wealth is distributed within a country. In many of the poorest countries, there is a huge gap between the richest and poorest members of society. Even in developed countries, there's often a very uneven distribution of wealth. In a free market, inequality is almost inevitable. Some economists see that as a failing of the market system and argue that it results in an unfair society. Others argue that it's not necessarily a bad thing, as it rewards people who work hard and encourages them to be more productive and come up with new ideas.

> THERE IS ALL THE **DIFFERENCE** IN THE WORLD BETWEEN TREATING PEOPLE **EQUALLY** AND ATTEMPTING TO MAKE THEM EQUAL.
>
> **FRIEDRICH HAYEK**

As with many economic ideas, both sides of the argument have some truth in them, and the solution in practice is often a compromise between the opposing views.

A growing gap

Free markets not only create inequality, but can also increase it. Successful businesses use their profits to become even more productive, and so more competitive. Rich people can invest their money in businesses and get richer, but those without resources lag further and further behind. In many rich countries, this is seen as a social problem, and some governments have introduced progressive taxes, taking a bigger portion from higher incomes, and helping those on low incomes with welfare benefits and a minimum wage. Economists suggest countries with a narrower range of incomes from rich to poor and less inequality not only have fewer social problems, but also more successful and stable economies. But in countries such the US and UK, governments believe the economy does best if incomes are set by the markets. The gap between rich and poor is greater than

MILTON FRIEDMAN (1912–2006)

Born in Brooklyn, New York, Friedman earned a Ph.D. in economics. He worked in New York and Washington and taught at the University of Chicago. The ideas he developed there, recommending low taxes and unregulated markets, made him probably the most influential economist of the late 20th century, working as an adviser to presidents Nixon and Reagan.

SOME HIGHLY PAID JOBS OFFER EXTRA BENEFITS AND BONUSES AS WELL AS SALARIES THAT ARE MANY TIMES HIGHER

What are you worth?
Not all jobs pay the same. Bankers, for example, earn far more than nurses, even though nurses provide an essential service. This is because in a free market, bankers are valued as creators of wealth.

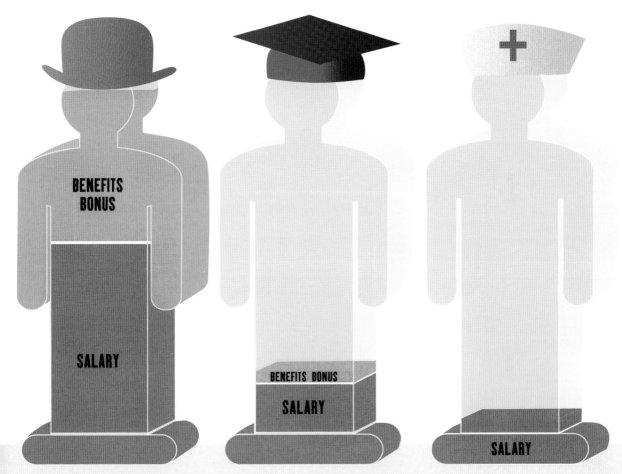

BENEFITS BONUS

SALARY

BENEFITS BONUS

SALARY

SALARY

elsewhere in the developed world, and is widening. Managers of large companies can earn many times more than their workers, and bankers make fortunes, while their cleaners may live in relative poverty. This inequality is justified by the "trickle down" theory: that bankers and businesspeople should be rewarded most because they create wealth that benefits us all.

Give everyone a chance
Supporters of free markets argue that more socialist policies curb people's freedom in order to achieve equality. Instead of trying to make everybody's income equal, they say that we should offer social mobility, so that it's easier for people to climb the social ladder and earn what they deserve. To do this, everyone—no matter what their background, gender, or ethnicity—should be offered equal opportunities to succeed, through equal access to education and jobs. Although the outcome will still be an unequal distribution of wealth, this determination to offer equal opportunity to all ensures a much fairer society.

See also: 126–127

THE COST OF BORROWING

Most people who need money can borrow it, then pay it back with interest. But people on low incomes, who need it most and can't guarantee repayment may end up paying more to borrow money than richer people. Often "loan sharks"— who are illegal lenders—take advantage of the poor and charge huge rates of interest.

THE BIG MAC INDEX

It's hard to compare the cost of living in different countries, because how much you can buy with each currency differs. However, the British *Economist* magazine does this by using a "Big Mac Index," which compares the price of a product that's the same worldwide—the McDonalds Big Mac burger.

Living standards and inequality
IN PRACTICE

PAYING THE PRICE

Many shoppers look for the best quality goods at the lowest prices, without thinking about where the goods come from. But consumers are now aware that fashionable clothes and sports gear are cheap because they're made in sweatshops using forced labor and child workers, and they are prepared to pay a little more to stop this exploitation.

DEAD-END JOBS

Industries in the growing service sector have created jobs, but many of these vacancies are poorly paid, in places like stores, call centers, or fast-food restaurants. They offer little chance of promotion or job security, and so are considered temporary dead-end jobs, not careers for life.

Some families are more privileged than others. Those "born with a silver spoon in their mouth" have an economic advantage from the start, since their connections and money help them to get better jobs and even more money. It may seem unfair, but would it be fair to take it away from them? Aren't families entitled to offer their children the best possible opportunities?

THAT'S **NOT FAIR!**

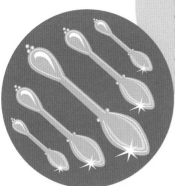

STANDARD OF LIVING

Standards of living differ around the world, and within countries. The developed world tends to have a higher standard of living, but some countries have large populations with high levels of inequality, while some small countries, such as Brunei, may be rich in resources such as oil, that bring a high standard of living to most of its population.

Advances in technology, economic development, and growth in the markets have brought unprecedented wealth to much of the world. But not everyone has benefitted equally. In many countries, most of the population lives in poverty, and even in some developed countries the gap between rich and poor is widening.

With the advent of mass media, people are aware of the effects of poverty around the world and are anxious to help. Many people give to charities, especially after news of a natural disaster. Charity events like Band Aid concerts raise large sums of money, but compared with the continuing need, this is a drop in the ocean.

FIRST AID

PHILANTHROPY

While billions of people live in poverty, there are a few who are multibillionaires. Many of the super-rich believe it's their duty to be philanthropic, to give some of their wealth to charity. This may seem generous, but it's often only a very small proportion of their wealth, which may not be targeted carefully to where it could be most effective.

What's in your POCKET?

Finding a BALANCE

Earning a LIVING

A SAFE place for my money

Do you REALLY need that?

Looking after the PENNIES

Buy NOW, pay later?

How would you like to PAY?

Travel MONEY

For a RAINY day...

Making PLANS

Managing your personal finances, running a household budget and generally looking after your money involves the same economic principles as running a business. How much you spend, what you buy and where you shop are all economic decisions. So, too, are the choices you make about your job, your leisure pursuits, and your plans for the future.

Finding a **BALANCE**

IN ORDER TO PAY FOR THE THINGS THAT WE NEED AND WANT, WE MUST HAVE MONEY. AND MOST PEOPLE NEED TO WORK TO EARN THAT MONEY. TO FIND A BALANCE BETWEEN WHAT WE HAVE TO DO, AND WHAT WE WOULD LIKE TO DO, WE HAVE TO MAKE DECISIONS ABOUT WHAT KIND OF WORK TO DO, AND HOW MUCH TIME TO SPEND AT WORK.

> MY FAVORITE THINGS IN LIFE DON'T COST ANY MONEY. IT'S REALLY CLEAR THAT THE MOST PRECIOUS RESOURCE WE ALL HAVE IS TIME.
>
> STEVE JOBS, CO-FOUNDER OF APPLE INC.

All work and no play...

The decisions we make about work are economic decisions. The time we have is a resource that can be used in many ways. Some of it's already taken up with things we absolutely have to do, such as sleeping and eating. The rest, roughly two-thirds of our time, is available for either work or leisure and to lead a full and happy life. It's important to find a balance. For many people in poor countries, the choices they have are limited, and in order to get the necessities of life they must work long hours for little pay, leaving them with neither the time nor money for leisure. But in developed countries, most people choose their lifestyle and the work–life balance that suits them.

Is it worth it?

Of course, choosing what work to do depends on how much money we can earn, and whether that will pay for everything that we want as well as need. But working also involves a large proportion of our time. Achieving the work–life balance we want is an example of what economists call "opportunity cost" (see pp. 40–41)—this means measuring the value of things we want by what we are prepared to give up for them. The income from a job is valuable to us, but then so is our leisure time. If we work more, we may have more income, but this comes at the cost of less leisure time.

CAREER...

On the other hand, if we choose to spend more time enjoying our leisure activities, we are left with less opportunity to earn money.

Time and opportunity

Time isn't the only resource that we have. There are also other factors that affect our choice of what kind of work to do, including education, skills, and experience. These in turn affect the opportunities that are available to us. We can decide to learn new skills, and get better qualifications in order to apply for jobs with higher salaries. Again, it's a matter of finding the balance between the extra work we have to put in and the lifestyle we would like to achieve—whether we want a big house and car, or are happier to have more leisure time to play sports or pursue hobbies.

It's up to you

There are other factors involved in choosing a career. While some people live to work, others work to live. Some have an ambition to become a doctor or a lawyer, for example, while others see work as simply a way of making enough money to pay for what they need and want. And while some

WORK OR STUDY?

Choosing whether or not to go to college also involves an opportunity cost. Instead of the four or more years you spend studying and the tuition involved, you could get a job and earn money. On the other hand, with a college degree you likely have a better chance of getting the job you want, and probably a better salary in the long term.

people enjoy their jobs and are happy to spend long hours at work, many people want to work as little as is necessary. In the end, the choice of what work we do, including how much money we can earn and how much of our time it will take up, is an economic one. To lead the life we would like, we must use our resources to provide us with the things we want and the time to enjoy them. We have to match our income to the lifestyle we have chosen.

On average, full-time workers in developed countries spend about 40% of their time at work.

WHICH IS MORE IMPORTANT?   ... LIFESTYLE

⬆ Work–life balance
We need to work to pay for the things we want in life. But this must be balanced against the need for enough leisure time in which to enjoy them.

See also: 56–57 126–127

Earning a LIVING

VERY FEW PEOPLE HAVE SO MUCH MONEY THAT THEY DON'T EVER HAVE TO WORK. AT SOME STAGE, ALMOST ALL OF US WILL HAVE TO THINK ABOUT HOW WE WILL EARN A LIVING. IN ADDITION TO DECIDING WHAT KIND OF WORK WOULD SUIT US BEST, WE HAVE TO MAKE DECISIONS ABOUT GETTING A JOB OR PERHAPS STARTING A BUSINESS OF OUR OWN.

> EACH MAN **DELIGHTS** IN THE **WORK** THAT SUITS **HIM** BEST.
> HOMER, ANCIENT GREEK WRITER

UNEMPLOYMENT

It's not always possible to find work. Sometimes there are a lot more people than there are jobs available. And even if you have a job, you could lose it if the company isn't doing well. It's not easy coping when you're unemployed, but most governments have programs to help people who are out of work pay their bills and find new employment.

Pay your way

As young people grow up and finish their education, they need to become financially independent from their parents, and to pay for the things that they need and want themselves. Ideally, they want to be doing work that they will enjoy, and that uses their skills and knowledge, but it's likely that the main reason for going to work is to earn money.

For most people, this means finding employment—getting a job, and being paid by an employer for the work you do. Employers normally advertise when they have job vacancies to fill and are hiring new workers. Someone looking for employment can see if the job might be suitable for them, but also how much it pays. The employer may be offering wages in a number of different ways—at a certain amount per hour, or per day, so that how much you can earn depends on the number of hours you work. Or it may be in the form of a salary of a certain amount per year.

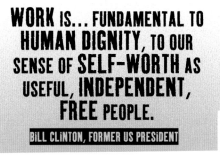

WORK IS... FUNDAMENTAL TO HUMAN DIGNITY, TO OUR SENSE OF SELF-WORTH AS USEFUL, INDEPENDENT, FREE PEOPLE.

BILL CLINTON, FORMER US PRESIDENT

CLIMBING THE CAREER LADDER

The career ladder ❯
Throughout their working lives, workers can get promoted and make their way up the career ladder by gaining additional knowledge and skills.

A good prospect

It's not simply the wages or salary that an employer is offering that matters though. Although everyone wants to be paid well, young people, in particular, may choose to work for lower wages if they can learn new skills and gain experience on the job. Most people start their working lives in jobs that aren't well paid, or in apprenticeship programs, or even unpaid internships, and then work their way up the career ladder. So, when they're looking for a job, they consider whether it offers them the chance of promotion, or will be good for their job prospects in the future.

In the European Union in 2014, 70% of working-age men were employed, compared with 60% of working-age women.

Work and home

Traditionally, it was the man of the house who was the "breadwinner"—earning money for all the family—and in many cultures, women have been expected to stay at home and do "women's work," such as cooking, cleaning, and bringing up children. But today, especially in richer developed countries, most women go out to work, and more are taking on jobs that were previously considered "men's work." Economists are recognizing that women who do housework do actually have a job,

but that it's unpaid work. Now that many women are going out to work, couples often share the housework, or may pay for someone else to do it.

One way of balancing the demands of home and work is to take a part-time job. Although this was an option for mothers, so that they had time for looking after children, it's becoming more common for men, too. Some employers even allow "job-sharing," where one job is divided between two or more people. Working fewer hours per day, or fewer days per week, gives more time for family or other interests, but of course, means less income, and may not be possible for everyone.

Be the boss

Not everyone who works is employed. Many people are self-employed, running their own businesses, or in partnership with colleagues. There are advantages to being your own boss, such as making decisions for yourself, and enjoying the profits when the business does well. But running a business can involve long hours of hard work, and doesn't guarantee a regular income.

See also: 56–57, 124–125

A **SAFE** place for my money

ONCE YOU HAVE A JOB OR RUN A BUSINESS, YOU HAVE TO THINK ABOUT WHAT TO DO WITH THE MONEY YOU EARN. IF IT'S IN CASH, YOU COULD PUT IT IN YOUR POCKET OR KEEP IT UNDER THE MATTRESS. BUT, OF COURSE, IT WOULD BE SAFER IN A BANK, AND THERE ARE OTHER ADVANTAGES. A BANK ACCOUNT GIVES YOU FLEXIBILTY, OFFERING CREDIT WHEN NEEDED OR HELPING YOUR MONEY TO GROW.

> **IF YOU WOULD BE WEALTHY, THINK OF SAVING AS WELL AS GETTING.**
> BENJAMIN FRANKLIN

Safe and secure

Perhaps the first thing people think of when they decide to open a bank account is that it's a safe place to keep their money, locked away in the vaults of a secure building. But today there's comparatively little cash in the banks, and the accounts consist of numbers in a computer program—but it's still safer than having the cash in your pocket. The main reason most people have a bank account is for convenience.

Although some people still get paid at the end of the week or month in cash or by check, which they can deposit into the bank, more and more employers transfer their workers' pay directly into their bank accounts. And while small businesses are often paid in cash for their goods or services, customers are increasingly choosing to buy things using debit or credit cards. So, for most people earning money, it's essential to have a bank account.

Easy access

In addition to providing a place to put your income, banks offer different ways of dealing with your expenditure: the things you need to pay for. You can withdraw money, either over the counter at a branch of your bank, or from an ATM (automated teller machine). But you can also use your bank card to pay for things, in stores, by phone, or online. And you can ask the bank to make regular payments, such as rent or loan repayments, direct from your account. To help you track what's going in and out of your account, most banks have an online banking service, where you can see how much you have in your account, and manage your money.

Another advantage is that banks can lend money to their customers, to cover unexpected expenses, or to pay for major purchases. This might be in the form of an overdraft, allowing you to spend more money than

FINANCIAL ADVICE

Banks often offer many different ways of saving or investing, and will help you decide which option is best for you. But, of course, a bank will want you to save with them, not another bank.

So, it's a good idea to use an independent financial adviser, a professional who can compare all the services available from different banks, and decide which you should choose.

WHAT CAN I DO WITH THE MONEY I EARN?

INVEST
Investing money either in your own business, or as a shareholder, can be profitable but involves some risk.

SAVE
Regularly putting money into a savings account means your money will grow, giving you funds for the future.

SPEND
It's useful to have some money available to buy things when you need them, or when prices are low.

INVEST

SAVE

SPEND

Spare money
If you're careful, you may have some money to spare from your income after you have paid for all the necessities. It's up to you to decide whether you spend, invest, or save it.

you have in your account, for which the bank charges a fee, or in the form of a loan that has to be paid back, with interest, in regular installments.

Using the leftovers
If you earn enough money to cover all your expenses and have some left over, you may wonder what's best to do with it. You could spend it, treating yourself to something you've always wanted, or keep it in your bank account for when it's needed. If you choose to save your money for the future, there are better options than a simple bank account. Most banks offer savings accounts, for instance, which give a better rate of interest than their ordinary accounts, so long as you keep your money in them for a set period of time. Putting money into one of these accounts will

keep it safe, but also means that it's guaranteed to grow. Or you could invest your money by buying shares in a business (see pp. 100–101), or putting it into an investment fund, which buys and sells shares and other financial products on its customers' behalf. This may bring greater returns for your money, but it is riskier than keeping it in the bank so it's best to seek financial advice before deciding.

See also: 102–103, 142–143

AN INVESTMENT IN KNOWLEDGE PAYS THE BEST INTEREST.
BENJAMIN FRANKLIN

See also: 58–59, 124–125

Do you REALLY

THERE ARE ALL KINDS OF THINGS THAT YOU CAN SPEND YOUR MONEY ON. SOME, SUCH AS FOOD AND HOUSING, ARE ESSENTIAL, BUT THERE ARE OTHERS THAT ARE LESS IMPORTANT. TO MAKE SURE YOU LIVE WITHIN YOUR MEANS, NOT SPENDING MORE THAN YOU HAVE IN INCOME, YOU MUST KEEP A CAREFUL EYE ON WHERE YOUR MONEY IS GOING.

> ANNUAL INCOME TWENTY POUNDS, ANNUAL EXPENDITURE NINETEEN POUNDS NINETEEN AND SIX, RESULT **HAPPINESS.** ANNUAL INCOME TWENTY POUNDS, ANNUAL EXPENDITURE TWENTY POUNDS OUGHT AND SIX, RESULT **MISERY.**
>
> CHARLES DICKENS, ENGLISH AUTHOR OF DAVID COPPERFIELD

Coming in and going out

To make sure you live within your means, it's a good idea to work out a budget—a record of what expenses must be paid versus how much money is coming in. You can do this in a special account book or on a computer spreadsheet. Whichever method you choose, the idea is the same: you compare your income, such as your monthly wages, with your expenditure, the amount you spend in a month.

Needs and wants

If you have a job with a regular income, you know how much money you have in your budget, and that this will be the same each month. Next, you need to list the things that you spend money on, and how much they cost. The first things that you put on your list of expenses are the essentials, such as housing, food, and payments for gas, electricity, and water. Some are regular payments, the same every month, but others will be different at different times of the year. There may be other things that are important, such as phone bills, bus and train fares, and insurance payments. Next on your list will be things that maybe are not essential, but give you pleasure or make your life more comfortable. These include money you spend on your hobbies and leisure activities, such as sports, music, books, and seeing movies.

⟳ Shopping list

If you are careful about your everyday spending and stick to your list of priorities, you can afford to treat yourself from time to time with things you want but don't need.

THINGS YOU WANT...

need that?

Making the cut

When you add up all these payments, you can compare the total expenditure with your income. If your spending is more than your income, to balance your budget you must cut the amount you are spending on some things, or find a way of increasing your income, for example, by working longer hours or getting a better paying job. It's usually easier to make cuts in your spending than it is to increase your income. Because you have a list of the things that you spend money on, you can put them in order of priority and decide where you could make cuts, spend less, to balance your budget. At the top of the list are the things that you can't do without, and the expenses that have to be paid. Spending on these can sometimes be reduced, for instance, by walking to work instead of taking the bus, or by being more careful about using electricity. But it's the things lower down the list that you could manage without, especially the treats you buy for yourself, such as the latest gadgets or trendy clothes.

NO PLACE LIKE HOME

Probably the biggest regular expense for most people is paying for somewhere to live. Choosing whether to share with friends, rent a place of your own, or take out a mortgage to buy an apartment or house depends on your income. The amount you pay each month in rent or a mortgage will greatly affect the rest of your budget.

Leave some for fun!

By asking yourself if you really need some of these things, you can cut down on your expenditure, and work out a budget to enable you to live within your means, and even have some money left over that you can save. It needn't mean that you have to give up the things you enjoy. You can include some "fun money" in your budget to pay for treats such as nights out, club memberships, or vacations. If you make a wish list of things you want, rather than being tempted to buy them right away, you can get them when you can afford them—or maybe decide in the end that you don't really need them!

See also: 132–133, 144–145

THINGS YOU NEED...

Try not to spend more than 90% of your income. Aim to set aside at least 10% for any big expenses that come along.

Looking after the

NOBODY LIKES TO PAY MORE THAN THEY HAVE TO, ESPECIALLY IF THEY ARE TRYING TO STAY WITHIN A TIGHT BUDGET. WHILE YOU CAN KEEP COSTS DOWN BY DOING WITHOUT SOME LUXURIES, THERE ARE SOME THINGS THAT YOU HAVE TO BUY. BUT WITH A LITTLE THOUGHT AND PLANNING THERE ARE WAYS THAT YOU CAN REDUCE THE AMOUNT YOU SPEND ON NECESSITIES, TOO.

> **BEWARE OF LITTLE EXPENSES; A SMALL LEAK WILL SINK A GREAT SHIP.**
> BENJAMIN FRANKLIN

In the developed countries, around 220 lb (100 kg) of food per person is wasted each year.

Save every day

When you look at your expenditure, a list of the things you spend money on, you'll see that there are certain things, such as rent or loan repayments, that have to be paid regularly, and have a fixed cost that can't be reduced. But there are also lots of smaller expenses in your budget, which vary from time to time. There are items, such as clothes or furniture, that you only buy occasionally, but a large part of your spending is on day-to-day living expenses, including food, travel, and utilities like electricity and water. It's these everyday expenses that you can look to cut. It may seem like you can only make small savings on many of these expenses, amounting to only a few cents on each item, but over time these can add up to a significant reduction. Often, we buy and use things without thinking about their cost, and don't realize that there are cheaper alternatives, or that we are wasting money. With a bit of thought and forward planning, though, we can keep our spending down. For example, there are obvious ways to reduce consumption, like switching off electrical devices when they're not being used, or wearing warm clothes rather than turning up the heat.

Easy living

A lot of the things we spend money on are simply for convenience, to make life easier. It is cheaper, for example, to buy fresh food and cook it ourselves, rather than a packaged prepared meal or takeout. Having a car is also more convenient than using public transportation, but can be more expensive to run, and the latest smartphone may look cool, but is it much more useful than the one you already have?

Bagging a bargain ➜
Buying a big bag of apples, rather than getting them one by one, might save you money, but only if you eat them all before they go bad.

PENNIES

Small changes, big savings

But you don't have to make changes to your lifestyle to save money. In your regular grocery shopping, it pays to plan ahead and buy the cheaper economy sizes of some products, rather than simply buying things as and when you need them, and it's worth looking for special offers. It's also important to think about how much you really need, and whether you'll be able to use everything before its best-before date. Throwing away unused food is money down the drain, and a surprisingly large proportion of many people's expenditure. Beware, too, of being tempted by a bargain. If something seems too good to be true,

CONSUMER PROTECTION

Many countries have laws to protect consumers, ensuring they're not cheated when paying for goods and services. These laws prevent sellers from misleading customers, for example, by false claims in advertising, deceptive offers that aren't really cheaper, or packaging that appears to hold more than it actually does.

it often turns out to be a false economy. Especially when buying things like clothes, furniture, or electrical goods, it's often wise to spend a bit more to get something that will last longer. Take the time to shop around, and compare goods and prices. Above all, try to avoid buying something on impulse that you will regret later! Make a list of what you need and want, and then stick to it. The small savings you make on everyday purchases can help to keep you within your budget, and maybe give you a little extra money to spend on the things on your wish list.

Look after the pounds

According to the saying, if you look after the pennies, then the pounds will look after themselves. But you have to be just as careful when spending large amounts, too. The money you save on small purchases is wasted if, for example, you buy an expensive gym membership that you don't have the time to use.

See also: 128–129, 130–131

SOMETIMES WHAT LOOKS LIKE A BARGAIN...   IS A FALSE ECONOMY

See also: 116–117, 130–131

Buy now, pay

MANAGING A BUDGET IS A QUESTION OF LIVING WITHIN OUR MEANS, NOT SPENDING MORE THAN YOU CAN AFFORD. SOMETIMES, HOWEVER, THERE ARE THINGS YOU NEED, BUT DON'T HAVE ENOUGH MONEY FOR. YOU CAN PAY FOR THESE BY BORROWING MONEY, AND SPREADING THE COST BY REPAYING IT OVER A PERIOD OF TIME.

Saving up

Of course, it's sensible to keep your spending within your income. But some things are a major expense, and may well cost more than you have in the bank. They may be things, such as a car or a vacation abroad, that you can delay buying until you've saved enough money, but there may be other things that you need more urgently, like a repair, or that would take a very long time to save for. One way of paying for them is to borrow the money.

Home, sweet home

Young people in particular often face large expenses before they have started to earn any money. Many of them take on student loans, for example, to pay for their studies, which they can pay back once they have jobs. Others may borrow money to cover the costs of starting a business—making repayments as the business grows. But for most people, the biggest purchase they are likely to make is buying a place

Repayment plan

Some businesses that sell expensive items, like cars, offer credit so that customers can buy goods when they want them and spread the cost with a repayment plan.

CAR SALES

CREDIT RATING

Before lending money, banks check that the borrower is able to make the repayments. Normally, they will ask a company, known as a credit rating agency, to assess the borrower's financial history. This credit rating is based on the income and the property of the borrower, but also on their credit history—how well they have paid their debts in the past.

to live, and very few would be able to do this without borrowing money. A loan to buy a house or apartment is called a mortgage, and the bank will usually charge less for it than other kinds of borrowing, since the property is used as security. If you don't repay the loan, the bank can take your home away from you.

LATER?

BIG PURCHASES CAN BE PAID FOR OVER SEVERAL MONTHS OR YEARS...

EVERY TIME YOU BORROW MONEY, YOU'RE ROBBING YOUR FUTURE SELF.
NATHAN W. MORRIS, US AUTHOR

According to the US Federal Reserve, the average American household in 2015 owed $7,281 in credit card debt.

A matter of great interest

The advantage of borrowing money is that you can have the things that you need or want right away, but spread the cost over a set period of time by making regular repayments. The major disadvantage of borrowing is that the lender, usually a bank, will charge you interest on the loan. This means that you end up paying back more money than you originally borrowed. And it could even be more than double the amount. This is because a loan is normally repaid over several years, and the interest rate is per annum (meaning per year, and often abbreviated to "pa"). The lender charges interest not just on the original amount of the loan, but each year on the total amount that's still owed, plus any interest on top of that. In addition to loans

for major purchases such as a house, banks offer other ways of borrowing money. For example, if you have an unexpected expense such as repairs to your car and don't have enough money to pay for them, your bank may offer you an overdraft. This allows you to take more money from your account than you have in it, up to a specified amount, and pay the money back when you can.

Paying with plastic

An alternative is to use credit for purchases, paying by credit card for an unmissable bargain, for example, or to book a vacation when prices are low. As with other forms of borrowing, credit cards can be a useful way of deferring payment to a later date, but they have their downside, too. If you don't pay back the full amount you've used quickly, you will be charged a high rate of interest on what you still owe, and the debt will grow. With all forms of borrowing, it's important to budget for regular repayments to keep from getting yourself deeper and deeper into debt.

See also: 138–139

THE RATE FOR THE JOB

IN A FREE MARKET, HOW MUCH PEOPLE ARE PAID DEPENDS ON SUPPLY AND DEMAND. LAWYERS, FOR EXAMPLE, MIGHT BE HIGHLY PAID BECAUSE FEW PEOPLE HAVE THE SKILLS REQUIRED AND PEOPLE WILL PAY A LOT FOR THEIR SERVICES. CAFÉ WORKERS MIGHT BE POORLY PAID BECAUSE LOTS OF PEOPLE CAN DO THE JOB AND THE PROFITS FROM SELLING COFFEE ARE SMALL. BUT IN PRACTICE IT'S NOT ALWAYS THIS SIMPLE.

WAGE SLAVES

Manual and unskilled workers are usually at the bottom of the pay scale. They've little bargaining power since there are many of them and they're easily replaced. To be competitive, companies buy unskilled or manual labor at the lowest cost. They may also try to replace laborers by machines or cheaper foreign workers. Employment in the unskilled sector is often precarious, with workers hired on short-term contracts and let go when business is slack.

GENDER PAY GAP

In theory, men and women should have equal bargaining power when competing for the same job. In practice, women often get significantly less pay, typically more than 20 percent less in the US. Laws have been introduced to lessen this gender pay gap, but it's still there. Various explanations have been given for this situation, but the most likely is the most obvious: sex discrimination.

CORPORATE CEO

"People who work **sitting** down get paid more than people who work **standing** up."

OGDEN NASH, US POET

TOP PAY

In the past, the highest paid people were professionals such as doctors and lawyers. The long training and level of skill involved meant that there were fewer of them. In recent years, professionals have been left behind by celebrities, business leaders, and people working in the financial industries—due to bonuses and commissions. In the UK in 2015, brokers earned on average $184,000 annually. That compares with $115,700 per year for senior doctors.

CEOs of the top 100 companies in the UK earn about 183 times more than a full-time worker on the average wage.

AIRLINE PILOT

CONSTRUCTION WORKER

DIRTY WORK

Some people do dirty, unpleasant, and even dangerous work—often enduring long hours in bad conditions. Mostly, this is because they have no other choice, and in such cases the worst work is often the worst paid. In many developing countries, even children may be forced to work for dreadful pay in terrible conditions, making cheap goods in sweatshops and factories where there is little regard for their safety.

⊕ Pay variation
Business and banking executives are well rewarded in developed countries. Some professionals earn a good salary, but unskilled workers can be vulnerable to downturns in the economy.

⏻ Credit card
Effectively a quick and easy way to borrow money to make a purchase, a credit card is useful but the loan has to be paid back quickly to avoid high charges.

⏻ Debit card
When you pay for something with a debit card, the money is taken directly from your bank account and transferred straight into the account of whomever you are paying.

YOU CAN PAY FOR MOST THINGS USING A CARD OR EVEN YOUR SMARTPHONE

How would you

FOR MUCH OF HISTORY, PEOPLE HAVE USED CASH, COINS, AND BANKNOTES TO PAY FOR GOODS AND SERVICES. BUT GRADUALLY A RANGE OF ALTERNATIVE WAYS OF PAYING HAS EMERGED, INCLUDING DEBIT AND CREDIT CARDS AND ELECTRONIC MONEY TRANSFERS. IN THE 21ST CENTURY, TRANSACTIONS WITHOUT CASH, EVEN FOR SMALL AMOUNTS, ARE FAST BECOMING THE NORM.

> **MONEY IS JUST THE POOR MAN'S CREDIT CARD.**
> MARSHALL MCLUHAN, CANADIAN COMMUNICATIONS THEORIST

withdraw spending money from time to time, either by visiting your bank, or from an ATM (automated teller machine) using your debit or credit card.

See also: 12–13, 22–23

Cash in hand
The shift to a cashless society is now well under way, but banknotes and coins are still widely used—especially for paying out small amounts such as when buying a newspaper or a cup of coffee. Many small businesses, especially in less developed parts of the world, also don't have the facilities to deal with payments other than in cash. So, although it's no longer necessary to have large sums of money when you go out, you'll probably need to have some cash in your pocket. And if, like most people, your money is in the bank, you'll need to

Holding all the cards
It's these cards, and the technology behind them, that have revolutionized the way we pay for things today. In addition to using cards to withdraw cash from an ATM, you can use them to pay for things directly, and to pay for things that you order on the phone, or online. Stores and businesses worldwide now accept debit and credit cards in payment, and some stores even issue their own credit cards—known as store cards—which can be used to buy things from them. Modern cards are made from plastic—paying by card is sometimes referred to as "using plastic"—with magnetic strips or electronic chips embedded in them, which can be read by a store's card machine.

Phone app
Banking apps can be used to access funds just like a credit or debit card, but because transactions aren't confirmed with a PIN, they may be restricted to small amounts for security reasons.

3

Cash
Many people still prefer to pay with cash, especially for small purchases, and some small businesses aren't able to accept card payments.

4

like to PAY?

Once you have verified the transaction by entering your PIN (personal identification number), the machine instructs your bank to transfer money into the store's account. Using a debit card will take money from your account to make the payment, so long as you have enough money to cover the purchase. Using a credit card is different, since the bank is effectively lending you the money for that transaction, and it will have to be paid back at some time. Recently, a new generation of "smart cards" has appeared that contain an electronic chip that can communicate with a terminal via radio waves. This has allowed superfast "contactless" payment—simply putting the card very close to the terminal rather than inserting it. Similar technology has also produced apps for smartphones, so that they can be used in contactless transactions, replacing cards altogether.

Online
There are other ways you can make payments without cash or cards. You can instruct your bank to make payments straight from your account, by direct debit, to pay for things such as telephone and electricity bills, or set up a regular payment, for example, for your monthly rent. Most banks these days also offer an online banking service that allows account holders to manage their money through their home computers, tablets, or smartphones. On a secure website, you can see how much money you have in your account, but also make payments by transferring money directly from your account into someone else's, so long as you have their bank details.

ONLINE PAYMENT
Many companies now do business through the internet rather than in stores. You can order all kinds of goods and services online and have them delivered to your home. These can be paid for by debit or credit card, or by transferring money electronically from your bank account using an online payment company such as PayPal.

Travel MONEY

See also: 20–21

IT HAS BECOME EASIER AND CHEAPER
THAN EVER BEFORE TO VISIT OTHER COUNTRIES.
MANY PEOPLE TRAVEL ABROAD REGULARLY FOR
VACATION, TO VISIT FRIENDS AND RELATIVES, OR
ON BUSINESS; SOME PEOPLE EVEN CHOOSE TO
LIVE IN ANOTHER COUNTRY TO WORK OR STUDY.
EXPERIENCING A DIFFERENT CULTURE CAN BE EXCITING
AND REWARDING, BUT DEALING WITH DIFFERENT
CURRENCIES CAN SOMETIMES BE CHALLENGING.

ONE'S DESTINATION IS NEVER A PLACE BUT A NEW WAY OF SEEING THINGS.

HENRY MILLER, AMERICAN WRITER

Vacation money

There are almost 200 countries in the world, and most have their
own currency. Only a few, such as the 19 European countries of
the Eurozone, share a single currency, so it's almost inevitable
that if you travel to a foreign country, people there will use
different money from yours. In a very few places, stores and
businesses will accept other major currencies such as US
dollars or euros, but everywhere else, if you want to buy
something you'll have to pay in the local currency. So, you'll have
to change money into the currency of the country you are visiting.
You can do this at most banks, or at a currency exchange
office. But what you may not realize, is that you cannot
exchange your money for the same amount in the other
currency. The bank or *bureau de change* will charge
you for making the transaction, and this is normally
a percentage of the money you are changing.

CHANGING MONEY BEFORE YOU TRAVEL ABROAD COSTS MONEY

The
euro coins minted
in various countries
look different, but can
be used anywhere in
the Eurozone.

Currency costs

If you have some British pounds, for example, which you want to change into US dollars, the official exchange rate may be £1 = $1.50, but the *bureau* sells at a lower rate, and buys at a higher rate. So when you go to change your money, the bank will offer you perhaps only $1.40 for each of your pounds, effectively making 10¢ on the deal. But when get back from your trip and want to change some dollars back into pounds, the bureau will buy perhaps $1.60 from you for £1, 10¢ more than the exchange rate. The cost of changing money varies from place to place, from as low as 5 percent to as much as 15 or even 20 percent, and is often more expensive in airports and tourist areas than in banks and post offices. Exchange rates are constantly changing, too, so it can save you money if you plan ahead and change money when the rate is in your favor, at a bank that you can trust to give you a good deal.

Fantastic plastic

There are alternatives to buying cash for your travels. Debit and credit cards are widely accepted around the world, and they can be used to pay for things such as hotels, restaurants, and souvenirs. There are also prepaid debit cards, onto which you can put the amount of money you will need before you travel. You'll probably still need cash for smaller purchases and, just like at home, you can get this from an ATM using your debit or credit card. Unfortunately, this doesn't mean that you escape the cost of changing money. Your bank will likely charge for any payments you make in another currency, as well as using an exchange rate that is favorable to them, and this charge will also apply to any local currency you withdraw from an ATM.

You may even pay exchange costs without ever leaving home! If you buy things from another country online, for example, the seller will want to be paid in his or her own currency, and your bank will charge you for the transaction. If you are running a business with customers or suppliers in other countries, the cost of accepting or making payments in different currencies must be taken into account, and is reflected in the prices charged.

BUREAUX DE CHANGE

In addition to banks, and some post offices, there are companies that specialize in changing money. These currency exchanges, or *bureaux de change*, operate especially in tourist areas and city centers, and at airports and railway stations. They usually display a list of the currencies they deal with, alongside the prices, in the local currency, at which they buy and sell them.

For a RAINY

FROM AN EARLY AGE, WE ARE ENCOURAGED NOT TO SPEND OUR MONEY BUT TO SAVE IT UNTIL WE HAVE ENOUGH FOR THE THINGS WE WANT. AS WE GROW UP AND HAVE TO PAY FOR EVERYDAY EXPENSES THERE'S OFTEN VERY LITTLE LEFT OVER FROM OUR INCOME—BUT IF SAVED CAREFULLY, EVEN A SMALL AMOUNT CAN GROW INTO A USEFUL SUM.

Somewhere safe

Children the world over are taught that it's wise to save money rather than spend it, to put at least some of their money somewhere safe for the future. By putting a little bit of money away regularly, the savings gradually mount up, so that in time there'll be enough to pay for things that you wouldn't normally be able to afford. Another reason for saving is to have some money in case of emergencies, unexpected expenses such as repairing or replacing a faulty computer. The image of a piggy bank is a familiar one, and is often used to represent the idea of saving, but there are better ways of saving than putting money to one side, especially if it's more than just a few coins. For one thing, your money will be safer from theft in a bank, but more importantly the bank will pay interest on any money you save, helping it to grow more quickly.

See also: 128–129

> **IF YOU WOULD BE WEALTHY THINK OF SAVING AS WELL AS GETTING.**
> **BENJAMIN FRANKLIN**

Growing your money

There are many different types of bank account, and some of them are specifically designed for savers. These tend to offer the best rates of interest, which means that money is added to the funds in the account, by the bank, on a regular basis, usually monthly or yearly. For example, if you have a lump sum of $100, perhaps a gift or inheritance from a relative, that you want to save, you can put this into a savings account that pays

⊙ Initial investment

If you have $1,000 to save, you could put it into a savings account that offers an interest rate of, for example, 10% per year over a period of 10 years.

⊙ After 1 year

Your initial $1,000 has attracted 10% interest, $100, so now you have $1,100 in your account. In the next year it will grow by even more, 10% of $1,100, and so on.

⊙ After 5 years

Each year, your money grows, and you earn interest on the total amount, including previous interest. In five years, it has grown to $1,610.51.

HOW SAVINGS GROW OVER TIME...

day...

10 percent per year. After a year, the money will have grown by 10 percent to $110, but because this is what's called compound interest, the next year it will grow by 10 percent of $110, giving you an extra $11 rather than $10. There's a handy way to calculate the way money increases with compound interest, sometimes known as the "rule of 72." If the interest rate is x percent per year, then the amount will double every 72 divided by x years. So, if the interest rate is 8 percent per annum, for example, the money will have doubled after 9 years. And that is much better than keeping it in a piggy bank!

The first piggy banks, pots in the shape of a pig to save coins in, were made in Java, Indonesia, in the 14th century.

A fixed rate
In practice, interest rates vary over time, and the money in your account will grow according to the rates at the time the interest is worked out each year. Sometimes they will be higher than when you opened the account, and sometimes they'll be lower. To avoid the uncertainty, you may be able to open an account with a fixed rate of interest for a set period of time. However, if you do this and interest rates go up, you will lose out.

Losing interest
The longer you keep your money in an account, the more it will grow—and if you add to it by paying in more from time to time, it will grow faster. Banks offer the best interest rates if you agree not to withdraw your money for a period of time, say five or 10 years. While this means you'll end up with a larger lump sum at the end of the period, it also means the money isn't available for emergencies, or that you'll have to pay a penalty to access it before the end of the term. But it does also mean that you are less likely to be tempted to dip into your savings unless absolutely necessary.

See also: 144–145

❷ Final windfall
After seven years, the $1,000 you started out with has almost doubled, to $1,948.72. At the end of the 10-year period you will receive a total sum of $2,593.74.

BUYING TO INVEST
Most of the time, we buy the things that we need or want, and any money we have left over is put into savings. But some people use this money to buy things that they believe will increase in value, investments such as houses, gold and jewelry, works of art, or even fine wines.

... AND PROVIDE FOR THE FUTURE.

Making PLANS

THROUGHOUT OUR LIVES, WE MAKE DECISIONS ABOUT THE KIND OF LIFE WE WANT TO LEAD: WHAT JOB WE WILL DO, WHERE WE WILL LIVE, AND HOW WE WANT TO SPEND OUR MONEY. WHEN WE THINK ABOUT THE FUTURE, WE SHOULD REMEMBER THAT IT IS UNPREDICTABLE AND MAKE PLANS THAT ENSURE OUR SECURITY WHEN THINGS GO WRONG.

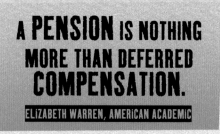

A PENSION IS NOTHING MORE THAN DEFERRED COMPENSATION.

ELIZABETH WARREN, AMERICAN ACADEMIC

Taking responsibility

Once a young person has left home to live independently, she starts to take on responsibilities. These include buying everyday things like food, clothes, and so on, as well as paying for somewhere to live and the household bills. And to meet these responsibilities, she will have to have an income, normally from a job or running a business. As she makes her way through life, she will probably take on more financial responsibilities, such as a mortgage to buy a house or apartment, or a loan to start her business, and these are often commitments to pay regular amounts over a period of years. It's fine to take on these kinds of commitments, so long as you have the income to pay for them. But the problems begin if you haven't made plans for when things might go wrong. You still have to pay the bills, even if something happens to your income. And if, like many people, you have also got a partner or even started a family, it will be a problem for all of them, too.

What it all goes wrong?

No one wants to believe that things could go wrong when planning the future, especially when it's something as important as taking on a new job, getting married, or buying a house. But bad things do happen, and you may lose your job through no fault of your own if the company you work for fails, or you can't work because of illness. In many countries, the government provides financial support for people

PLANNING AHEAD CAN HELP SECURE A ROSY FUTURE!

↻ **Looking ahead**
Life can be unpredictable, but planning ahead can go some way to making the journey more comfortable. Insurance and savings can provide funds for any financially difficult times and deal with unexpected expenses.

IT TAKES AS MUCH ENERGY TO WISH AS IT DOES TO PLAN.

ELEANOR ROOSEVELT, US POLITICIAN

who are sick or unemployed, funded by the taxes you pay when you're earning. But often this is barely enough to cover the basics. So, when making plans, it's wise to consider some insurance. This could be saving money regularly to provide emergency funds, however, an insurance policy will give you more security, and can be paid for in installments. When you take on a loan or mortgage, you can get insurance that will cover your expenses if you are unable to pay. There are also insurance policies to give you an income, and pay for medical care, if you become ill or have an accident, and life insurance that will provide your family with money if you die.

Growing older

As we age, our circumstances change. There will come a time when you'll want to stop work, but still need an income. Most governments provide a retirement pension, but this may not be enough

to live as comfortably as you've been used to. This can be supplemented with a private pension plan to give you an extra income in your retirement. Pensions are organized so that you make regular contributions while you're earning, and some employers also contribute to their workers' pensions.

While most of our plans are for the life ahead, we must also plan for what happens after we die. In addition to insurance to cover the commitments that we've taken on—which become the responsibility of those we leave behind—we have to consider what will happen to the money and property we own. What you own when you die, your estate, may be taxed but what is left can be passed on to your family and friends. Making a will, an official document recording your wishes, helps avoid legal arguments about who is entitled to your estate and the tax that you have to pay.

Legend has it that sailors and pirates used to wear gold earrings to pay for their funerals if they died at sea.

SETTING UP HOME

Sooner or later, most young people leave the family home to live independently. As they begin to earn regularly, this financial security enables them to take on the long-term commitments of setting up a home such as paying rent or repaying a mortgage. Many people want to have a family of their own and will have to consider the financial commitment of providing for their children for many years to come.

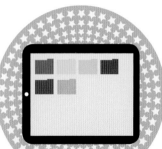

GETTING ORGANIZED

To manage your money and plan your budget properly, you need information about your income and expenditure. The key to this is keeping records of what you spend and how much you earn in an account book or on a computer—and remember to check your bank account regularly.

SAFE JOURNEY

Traveling abroad can be costly if something goes wrong. If you are delayed by weather, for example, you may have to pay more than you budgeted, and it's worse if you are robbed or need medical treatment. For protection, take out travel insurance before you go, either for a single trip or a policy to cover you whenever you go abroad.

Personal finances
IN PRACTICE

BE PREPARED

When you go to a bank to borrow money, they'll want to know if you'll be able to repay it, and whether you have security, such as a house, in case you default on the loan. You're more likely to be successful if you can give them the information they need, so prepare your case carefully before approaching the bank.

GET HELP

If you have some spare money, it can be difficult to know how best to save it. There are many different savings plans, so you may find it helpful to go to an independent financial adviser. Similarly, there are organizations that can help if you need advice about borrowing money or dealing with debt problems.

JOB MARKET

Unemployment rates among young people are often higher than for the rest of the population. Generally there are many young people applying for the same job. To be competitive in the labor market, and stand a chance of getting a good job, it helps to have educational qualifications and desirable skills that other applicants may lack.

INTERNET SECURITY

Banks and service providers try to make internet transactions secure using software and cryptography. But this won't protect your money unless you are careful, too. Keep your PINs and passwords secret, and only use sites you can trust. And just like your wallet, keep your smartphone safe, since it contains information valuable to hackers.

Managing your personal finances is a lot like running a business. To avoid getting into financial difficulties, you have to keep an eye on how much money is coming in and going out, and find ways of balancing that income and expenditure.

A HOME OF YOUR OWN

Most young people moving away from their family home live in rentals. At some stage they may decide to take out a mortgage to buy an apartment or house of their own. The advantage is that the property will belong to them, but it's also a responsibility, since they'll have to pay for its upkeep as well as repaying the loan.

JUST IN CASE

Most insurance is a sensible way of protecting yourself—it can be expensive if you're not insured when something goes wrong. Beware of persuasive salespeople and read the policy carefully. When buying electrical goods, for example, you may be offered insurance to cover theft or breakdown. If it costs as much as it would to replace the goods. it is probably not worth taking.

Directory of economists

Maurice Allais 1911-2010

French economist Maurice Allais was one of the early pioneers of behavioral economics, studying the psychology of decision-making and in particular how rational our economic behavior is when faced with several choices. He studied mathematics in Paris, and worked as an engineer before being appointed professor of Economics at the École Nationale Supérieure des Mines. He won the Nobel Prize for Economics in 1988.

Jean Bodin (1530–1596)

The son of a French tailor, Jean Bodin was a lawyer, historian, and influential political thinker. He also published one of the earliest studies of inflation. Linking the amount of goods to the amount of money in circulation, he blamed the rise in prices across Europe on the influx of silver and gold from Spanish colonies in South America, in the 16th century, when the population was growing.

Ha-Joon Chang (1963–)

South Korean Ha-Joon Chang works at the University of Cambridge, UK, and is a leading critic of mainstream economics and development policies. In books such as *Kicking Away the Ladder*, *Bad Samaritans*, and *23 Things They Don't Tell You About Capitalism*, he questions the impact of free trade and globalization and argues for alternative types of intervention to tackle poverty.

Antoine Augustin Cournot (1801–1877)

Although born into a relatively poor family, Antoine Cournot studied mathematics and became a tutor, a secretary to one of Napoleon's generals, and a university lecturer. He pioneered the use of mathematics in economics, compared the industrial output and profits of monopolies and duopolies, and was the first to draw a supply-and-demand curve on a graph to illustrate the link between the demand for an item and its price.

Gérard Debreu (1921–2004)

French mathematician Gérard Debreu traveled to the US in 1948 and joined the influential Cowles Commission at the University of Chicago to apply mathematics to economic issues. In 1983 he won the Nobel Prize for his work on equilibrium—how markets can achieve an efficient, fair, and stable balance between the demands of consumers and firms and the supply of goods and services.

Richard Easterlin (1926–)

US professor of economics Richard Easterlin set out his "Easterlin paradox" in 1974. Looking at surveys of people's happiness in 19 countries over three decades, he found that reported happiness increased with income, as expected, but didn't vary greatly across countries, despite differences in national income. Rich countries weren't always the happiest. The US saw increases in GDP from 1946 but a decline in happiness over the 1960s. This paradox sparked research into the link between economics and well-being.

Ernst Engel (1821–1896)

In 1885, German statistician Ernst Engel set out the "elasticity" of demand, showing how changes in income alter the level of demand. "Engel's law" showed that as people grow richer, they increase their spending on basic necessities—such as food—by less than their rise in income, but their spending on luxuries—such as vacations—grows at least as quickly as the rise in income.

Eugene Fama (1939–)

A third-generation Italian-American, Eugene Fama was the first in his family to go to college. In the 1960s, he showed that stock market price movements are impossible to predict in the short term, and that prices respond to new information almost instantly, which makes the market efficient. As the father of "efficient-markets theory," he won the Nobel Prize for Economics in 2013.

Milton Friedman (1912–2006) See p. 119

Ragnar Frisch (1895–1973)

Born in Norway, Ragnar Frisch originally trained as a goldsmith. A pioneer in the use of mathematics and statistics in economics, he coined the terms "econometrics," "microeconomics," and "macroeconomics." In 1932, he founded the Oslo Institute of Economics, and in 1969 he became the first recipient of the Nobel Prize for Economic Sciences, with his colleague Jan Tinbergen.

John Kenneth Galbraith (1908–2006)

John Kenneth Galbraith studied economics in Canada and the US. While teaching at the University of Cambridge, UK, he was greatly influenced by John Maynard Keynes (see p. 110). During World War II, he was deputy head of the US Government Office of Price Administration, but his support for permanent price controls led to his resignation. He worked as a journalist, academic, and economic adviser to President John F. Kennedy and gained a popular readership in 1958 with his book *The Affluent Society*.

Robert Giffen (1837–1910)

Giffen goods, commodities for which demand rises as prices rise, are named after Scottish financial journalist, statistician, and economist Sir Robert Giffen. The original Giffen good was bread (see p. 40), the staple of the poorest of British society in the 19th century. As the price of bread rose, the poor—who couldn't afford meat—spent more of their income on bread to survive. Demand increased because they had even less money for other food.

Friedrich Hayek (1899–1992) See p. 101

David Hume (1711–1776)

David Hume was one of the most influential British philosophers and economists of the 18th century. He entered Edinburgh University at the age of 12, and later lived in Paris and London before returning to Edinburgh. A prolific writer, he argued that economic freedom is essential for political freedom. He also showed that prices in a country alter with changes to its supply of money. Limiting imports and encouraging exports doesn't increase a country's wealth. Instead, as exports increase and more gold flows into the country to pay for them, prices for goods in that country actually rise.

William Jevons (1835–1882)
British economist William Jevons was a prolific writer on logic and economics. He showed that a commodity's value depends on its utility to the consumer, not on the cost of producing it. His idea of "marginal utility" explains consumer behavior. You enjoy the last chocolate you eat less than the first. The utility (value) of each extra chocolate—its marginal utility—decreases, so you'll only buy more if the price falls, or you'll buy a different product to get more utility.

Daniel Kahneman 1934– (and Amos Tversky 1937–1996) See p. 87

John Maynard Keynes (1883–1946) See p. 110

Paul Krugman (1953–)
US economist Paul Krugman is known for his pioneering work in international trade and finance and for his analysis of currency crises and fiscal (tax) policy. In 2008 he won the Nobel Prize for his study of international trade patterns, which is now known as new trade theory and places geography at the center of economics. He showed that the location of economic activity is driven by consumers' preference for a diverse choice of brands, producers' economies of scale, and the cost of transporting goods.

Arthur Laffer (1940–)
Laffer was one of a group of US economists who, in the 1970s, recommended less government interference with companies supplying goods and services. He is best known for the "Laffer curve," a graph of the relationship between tax rates and how much money they raise, which shows that increasing taxes beyond a certain level means the government may get less revenue.

Christine Lagarde (1956–)
Born in Paris, France, Christine Lagarde originally studied law and worked for an international firm of lawyers before following a career in politics. She became the French Minister of Commerce and Industry in 2005, and was later appointed as the Minister of Finance. In 2011, she was elected Managing Director of the International Monetary Fund.

Thomas Malthus (1766–1834)
English economist Thomas Malthus was the godson of philosophers David Hume and Jean-Jacques Rousseau, and went on to study at Cambridge University. He became a clergyman in the Church of England, but is most famous for his study of the connection between population growth and poverty. In 1805, he became the first ever Professor of Political Economy.

Alfred Marshall (1842–1924)
One of the most influential British economists and a founder of the neoclassical school, Marshall brought a scientific method to the study of economics. In his book *Principles of Economics*, he gave a comprehensive explanation of all aspects of the subject, and it became a standard textbook for students for more than 50 years. He taught at the universities of Bristol and Cambridge, and John Maynard Keynes (see p.110) was among the many students influenced by him.

Karl Marx (1818–1883) See p. 48

Carl Menger (1840–1921)
Born in Galicia, present-day Poland, Menger was a professor of economics at the University of Vienna, where he helped to develop the theory of marginal utility, explaining the value of goods in terms of each additional unit. His work on this led to a split from the prevailing German economic thinkers, and the founding of the Austrian school of economics with his colleagues Eugen Böhm von Bawerk, Friedrich von Wieser, and others.

John Stuart Mill (1806–1873)
Mill was born into a prominent English family of thinkers, and went on to become a philosopher, politician, and campaigner as well as an economist. His theories regarding the freedom of the individual from state intervention formed the basis for British 19th-century political and economic liberalism. He was a Member of Parliament in the 1860s, and was outspoken in his views about social justice. He was also an opponent of slavery, and with his wife Harriet Taylor he campaigned for women's rights.

Hyman Minsky (1919–1996)
Best known for his description of financial crises, and the "Minsky moment" (see p. 82) when a crash becomes inevitable, Hyman Minsky was a professor of economics at Washington University, St. Louis. His main interest was in the ups and downs of economies that can lead to "boom and bust." Influenced by J. M. Keynes, he recommended government intervention in financial markets.

Ludwig von Mises (1881–1973)
A leading economist of the Austrian School, von Mises studied under Eugen Böhm von Bawerk at the University of Vienna. He left Vienna for Geneva after the Nazis came to power in the 1930s, and eventually settled in New York, where he taught at the university. His anti-socialist economic theories were a major influence on Friedrich Hayek and the neoliberal economists in the US during the second half of the 20th century.

Franco Modigliani (1918–2003)
Modigliani, an outspoken antifascist and a Jew, left his native Italy in 1938 to escape the fascist dictatorship of Mussolini. He lived in Paris before settling in the US, where he taught economics. He went on to become a professor at the Massachusetts Institute of Technology. In 1985, he won the Nobel Prize for his study of savings and financial markets.

Dambisa Moyo (1969–)

A Zambian-born international economist now based in New York, Moyo is best known for her controversial opposition to aid for developing countries, expressed in her first book *Dead Aid*. She moved to the US to study, and later got her Ph.D. in Economics at Oxford. After working for the World Bank and Goldman Sachs she has devoted her time to writing and speaking about development and international economics, but is also on the board of several major companies, banks, and charities.

John Forbes Nash (1928–2015)

Joint winner of the 1994 Nobel Prize in Economic Science, John Nash was a brilliant mathematician whose work in "game theory" helped to explain the way that we interact with one another when making economic decisions. The Hollywood film *A Beautiful Mind* was based on his life, especially his struggles with schizophrenia.

Elinor Ostrom (1933–2012)

Elinor Ostrom was the first, and so far only, woman to win a Nobel Memorial Prize in Economic Sciences (which she shared with Oliver Williamson in 2009). She was born in Los Angeles, California, and after studying at UCLA taught at Indiana and Arizona State Universities, where she became known for her work on politics, government, and economics, and especially the production of public goods and services.

Vilfredo Pareto (1848–1923)

Although born in France, the son of a French mother and Italian father, Pareto was brought up in Italy, where he studied engineering and became a civil engineer. He later developed an interest in economics and sociology, and at the age of 45 became a professor of political economy at Lausanne University. He is best known for his work on welfare economics and income distribution, including the "Pareto efficiency" named after him.

Arthur Pigou (1877–1959)

A student of Alfred Marshall at Cambridge University, English economist Arthur Pigou developed the idea of extra taxes, called "Pigovian taxes" on businesses that create externalities, causing harm or cost to others. He became Professor of Political Economy at Cambridge in 1908, and remained there until 1943.

Robert Putnam (1941–)

US political scientist, Robert Putnam, has an interest in public policy and social change. In his book *Bowling Alone*, he studies the links between society and the economy, especially in the US. The social networks in society, which he calls "social capital," are a resource that he believes is dwindling in the modern world.

François Quesnay (1694–1774)

One of the first modern economists, François Quesnay was born in Méré, near Versailles, France. After studying medicine, he became a doctor in the King's court at Versailles, but later devoted his time to economics, writing his *Tableau Économique*, one of the first descriptions of the workings of the economy, in 1758.

David Ricardo (1772–1823) See p. 67

Joan Robinson (1903–1983)

One of the first successful female economists, Joan Robinson studied at Cambridge University, and after a period of traveling returned there to teach. There, she was influenced by John Maynard Keynes (see p. 110), and developed his ideas into her own theories of monetary economics, as well as reviving interest in Marxian economics. A great traveler, she also pioneered ideas of economic development.

Dani Rodrik (1957–)

Turkish economist Dani Rodrik studied economics in the US, where he is presently a professor of International Political Economy at Harvard University, but he retains strong links with his native Turkey. He is most influential in the fields of economic development and international economics, where he has closely examined the wide-ranging social and economic effects of increased globalization, and governments' responses to them.

Jeffrey Sachs (1954–)

Known for his work advising governments in Latin America and the former Communist countries of Eastern Europe and the Soviet Union in the 1980s and 90s, Jeffrey Sachs has more recently worked on issues of sustainable development and public health. He was born in Detroit, Michigan, and studied at Harvard University, where he also taught economics for more than 20 years. Since 2002 he has been director of the Earth Institute at Columbia University in New York.

Jean-Baptiste Say (1767–1832)

Best known for his description of supply and demand in the market, known as "Say's Law," French economist Jean-Baptiste Say was born in France, but finished his education in England. He worked as a merchant and later set up a cotton mill, but was also editor of a political magazine in Paris, popularizing the economic ideas of Adam Smith (see p. 32).

Joseph Schumpeter (1883–1950)

Born in Moravia, in what was then the Austro-Hungarian Empire, Joseph Schumpeter moved to Vienna as a child, where he studied at the university. He then went on to teach at the universities of Czernowitz (modern-day Ukraine) and Graz (Austria). After World War I he was appointed Austrian Minister of Finance, and later President of the Biedermann Bank, before moving to the US in 1924. Like Marx, (see p. 48) he believed that the capitalist system is destructive, but he described the innovations brought by capitalism as "creative destruction."

Amartya Sen (1933–)

Indian economist Amartya Sen was awarded the Nobel Prize in Economics in 1998 for his work in welfare economics, the study of how resources can best be allocated. He studied at the University of Calcutta (Kolkata) and then in Cambridge, UK, before taking up a career teaching at universities in India, the US, and the UK.

Herbert Simon (1916–2001)

A true polymath, Herbert Simon was a prominent thinker in many different fields, including psychology, sociology, computer science, and artificial intelligence—as well as politics and economics. Bringing together ideas from all these subjects, he was a pioneer of behavioral economics and especially the idea of "bounded rationality" (see p. 88), for which he was awarded the Nobel Prize for Economic Science in 1978.

Adam Smith (1723–1790) See p. 32

Nicholas Stern (1946–)

British economist Nicholas Stern is a former vice president of the World Bank, but is better known as an adviser to the British government on the economics of climate change. As the head of a team commissioned by the UK Treasury, he published the Stern Review Report on the Economics of Climate Change in 2006, which described climate change as "a result of the greatest market failure the world has seen."

George Stigler (1911–1991)

A leading member of the Chicago School of economics alongside Milton Friedman (see p. 119), George Stigler was a Nobel Prize winner in 1982. Born in Seattle, Washington, he studied at the University of Chicago, and after teaching at Columbia University in New York he returned to Chicago in 1958. In addition to his research into government behavior and the history of economics, Stigler was one of the first economists to explore the new field of information economics.

Joseph Stiglitz (1943–)

American economist Joseph Stiglitz became known for his work on information economics, and went on to become an economic adviser to President Bill Clinton in the 1990s, and then Chief Economist of the World Bank. He is critical of the prevailing free-market economics, and especially the way that globalization is managed by multinational companies and institutions such as the International Monetary Fund and World Bank.

James Tobin (1918–2002)

An economics adviser to President John F. Kennedy in the 1960s, James Tobin studied at Harvard, where he met John Maynard Keynes (see p. 110), and became an advocate of his economic policies. He was an expert on taxation, and suggested a tax, known as the "Tobin tax," on financial transactions to discourage reckless speculation in the financial markets.

Thorstein Veblen (1857–1929)

Brought up on a farm in Minnesota in a family of Norwegian immigrants, Thorstein Veblen rejected many of the mainstream views of economists of the time. He developed an unconventional approach, combining sociology and economics, which was critical of capitalism, and in The Theory of the Leisure Class he described the idea of "conspicuous consumption," and Veblen goods (see p. 59), which were named after him.

Léon Walras (1834–1910)

French economist Léon Walras studied engineering and tried several careers, including journalism and managing a bank, before turning to economics. He brought his background in mathematics to his study of economics when he was appointed Professor of Political Economy at the University of Lausanne in Switzerland, where he developed his theories of marginal value and the equilibrium of markets.

Marilyn Waring (1952–)

Politician and economist Marilyn Waring was born in Ngaruawahia, Waikato, New Zealand. She was elected to the New Zealand Parliament at the age of 23, but left politics in 1984 to pursue a career as an academic. Her book If Women Counted was a milestone in feminist economics, pointing out the way that mainstream economics ignored the contribution women make to the economy.

Beatrice Webb (1858–1943) and Sidney Webb (1859–1947)

Economist, historian, and activist Beatrice Webb and her husband, Sidney, were key figures in the British Trade Union movement, the cooperative movement, the socialist Fabian Society, and in the formation of the Labor Party—a major political party in the UK. Together, the Webbs campaigned for social reforms, including a minimum wage and the establishment of a welfare state. In addition to writing several books together, they were among the co-founders of the London School of Economics.

Max Weber (1864–1920)

Born in Erfurt, Germany, Max Weber was one of the founders of the modern study of sociology, teaching at several German universities. In his essay The Protestant Ethic and the Spirit of Capitalism, he described how the social and religious atmosphere in Northern Europe combined with capitalism and industrialization to bring about economic growth.

Friedrich von Wieser (1851–1926)

A prominent member of the Austrian School of economics, Friedrich von Wieser worked as a civil servant before becoming a professor at Vienna University. His contributions to economic theory include work on the idea of marginal utility (see p. 41) and the theories of value and the notion of opportunity cost.

Yanis Varoufakis (1961–)

Born in Athens, Greece, the self-styled "libertarian Marxist" Yanis Varoufakis studied mathematics in the UK before switching to economics for his Ph.D. From 1988 he taught at the University of Sydney, Australia, but returned to Greece in 2000, teaching at the University of Athens, and working as an adviser to the government. In 2015 he was appointed Finance Minister in the left-wing Syriza government, but resigned from this post after seven months. His departure was in protest against the austere terms imposed by international financial institutions on Greece in return for bailout loans (see p. 107).

Glossary

Asset
Things that someone owns that can be used as a resource, such as money, property, or equipment. Money that is to be received, including future payment for goods, or an outstanding debt, is also considered an asset.

Austrian School
Founded by Carl Menger in the late 19th century. This school of economics attributed all economic activity to the choices and actions of individuals, and opposed *government* intervention.

Balance of payments
The total of all money entering a country from abroad for *exports* less all money going out to pay for *imports* over a set period of time.

Balance of trade
The difference in the value of a country's *imports* and *exports* over a period.

Bankruptcy
A legal declaration that an individual or a company is unable to repay their *debts*.

Barter
A system of exchange in which *goods* or *services* are exchanged to pay for one another directly, without the use of a medium of exchange, such as money.

Bear market
A period of decline in the value of *shares* or other *commodities*. The opposite of a *bull market*.

Behavioral economics
A branch of economics that studies the effects of psychological and social factors on decisions.

Bond
A form of loan used to raise *capital*. Also known as securities, bonds are issued by a *government* or company in return for a sum of money; the bond issuer agrees to repay the borrowed sum plus *interest* at a date in the future.

Budget
A financial plan that lists all planned expenses and income.

Bull market
A period of increase in the value of *shares* or other *commodities*. The opposite of a *bear market*.

Capital
The means of production, the money and physical *assets* a business uses to produce goods and services and make an income.

Capitalism
An economic system in which the means of *production* are privately owned, companies compete to sell *goods* for a *profit*, and workers exchange their labor for a wage.

Cartel
Firms that cooperate in fixing the price of their *goods* or restricting their output to drive up the price.

Chicago School
A free-market group of economists, whose ideals of limiting the role of *government* and deregulation became mainstream in the 1980s.

Classical economics
Developed by Adam Smith and others, in the 18–20th century, this approach focused on the *growth* of nations and free *markets*, in which the pursuit of self-interest produces economic benefits for all.

Commodity
Any product or service that can be traded. Often refers to raw materials (such as oil or wheat), of roughly the same quality, whoever supplies them, that can be bought in bulk.

Communism
Invented by Karl Marx, a political and economic system of equality in which the property and the means of *production* are owned collectively. It is similar to *socialism*, and opposed to *capitalism*.

Company
A business in which two or more people work together to make a product or offer a service. Known also as "firms." Large companies are often referred to as *corporations*.

Competition

Competition arises when two or more producers try to win the business of a buyer by offering the best terms. More competition means that firms will be more efficient and prices lower.

Consumption

The purchase, and value, of *goods* or *services*. *Governments* add up individual purchases to calculate a figure of national consumption. The more resources a society consumes, the less money it puts into savings and *investments*.

Corporation

A *company* that's legally authorized to act as a single entity, and is owned by its shareholders who elect directors to run the business.

Cost of living

The average cost of basic needs, such as food and housing. It's a measure of how expensive it is to have an acceptable standard of life in different cities or countries.

Credit

A deferred payment. A creditor (lender) lends money to a debtor (borrower) who is trusted to pay later. A bank account is "in credit" when it has funds to repay its *debts*.

Debt

A promise made by one party (the debtor) to another (the creditor) to pay back a loan.

Default

The failure to repay a loan under the terms agreed.

Deficit

An imbalance. A trade deficit is an excess of *imports* over *exports*. A *government budget* deficit is an excess of public spending over *tax revenues*. The opposite of *surplus*.

Deflation

A persistent fall in the price of *goods* and *services* over time. The opposite of *inflation*.

Demand

The amount of *goods* or *services* that a person or group of people is willing and able to buy. The greater the demand, the higher the price.

Depression

A severe long-term decline in economic activity, in which *demand* and output slump, unemployment rises, and *credit* is scarce.

Development

The policies and *investment* by which a nation grows its economy and improves the well-being of its people—or seeks to assist others in poorer, developing countries.

Division of labor

The allocation of tasks to individuals or organizations according to their skills and resources, in order to improve efficiency and increase output.

Exports

The sale of *goods* and *services* to other countries. Opposite of *imports*.

Externality

A cost or benefit from an economic activity, which affects people not involved in that activity, and isn't reflected in its price. For example, noise from an airport may lower the value of nearby homes, but bees kept to produce honey may pollinate crops on a nearby farm.

Free-market economy

A *market* economy system in which decisions about *production* and prices are made by private individuals and companies, on the basis of *supply and demand*, with little or no *government* control.

Free trade

The *import* and *export* of *goods* and *services* without restrictions such as *tariffs* or *quotas* being imposed by *governments* or any other organizations.

GDP

Gross domestic product. A measure of national income over one year. GDP is calculated by adding up a country's annual output of *goods* and *services* and is often used to measure a country's economic activity and wealth.

Globalization

The free flow of money, *goods*, or people across international borders, leading to increasing integrated *markets* and further economic interdependence between countries.

GNP

Gross national product. Total value of all *goods* and *services* made in one year by a country's businesses, whether their *production* is based at home or abroad.

Goods
A term for physical products or raw materials that are sold to satisfy consumer *demand*.

Government
A system or process of running a country, or the people that run it. Economists debate government involvement in the economy.

Growth
An increase in the potential output of an economy over a period of time. It can be measured by comparing one country's *GDP* with another's, *per capita* (per head of population).

Hedge
Reducing risk by taking on a new risk to offset an existing one. Hedge funds are *investment* funds that pool *capital* from a limited number of wealthy, accredited individuals and institutions and invest it in a variety of *assets*.

Imports
The purchase of *goods* and *services* from other countries. The opposite of *exports*.

Industry
A general term for the *production* of *goods* or *services*. It is also used to describe a particular field, such as the oil industry or the film industry.

Inflation
A persistent rise in the price of *goods* and *services* over time. The opposite of *deflation*.

Interest
The cost of borrowing money. Interest payments reward lenders for the risk they take in lending their money to borrowers.

Interest rate
The price of borrowing money. The interest rate on a loan is generally stated as a percentage of the amount per year that must be repaid, in addition to the original sum of money borrowed.

Investment
An injection of *capital* aimed at increasing future *production* and *profits*.

Keynesianism
A school of economic thought in favor of *government* spending to pull economies out of *recession* and based on the ideas of the influential 20th-century economist John Maynard Keynes.

Laissez-faire
A French term that means "let it be," which is used to describe *markets* that are free from *government* intervention.

Macroeconomics
The study of the economy as a whole, looking at factors including *interest rates*, *inflation*, *growth*, and unemployment. An alternative field of study to *microeconomics*.

Market
A place, physical or virtual, where *goods* or *services* are bought and sold.

Mercantilism
A doctrine that dominated economics from the 16th–18th century. It emphasized *government* control over foreign trade to maintain a positive *balance of trade* and a plentiful *supply* of money.

Microeconomics
The study of specific details that together make up the economy, such as the economic behavior of households, firms, or *markets*. An alternative field of study to *macroeconomics*.

Monetary policy
Government policies aimed at changing the money *supply* or *interest rates*, in order to stimulate or slow down the economy.

Monopoly
A *market* in which there is only one firm. Free from *competition*, a firm generally produces a low output, which it then sells at a high price.

Mortgage
A loan based on the value of a property. The loan is used either to buy the property itself or the money can be used by its owner to raise funds for other purposes. If the borrower doesn't repay the loan, the lender can take and sell the property. A mortgage is a kind of *secured loan* with the property acting as the security.

Multinational
Operating in several countries. A multinational (or transnational) *corporation* is a large *company* that produces goods abroad.

Nationalization
The transfer of a firm or *industry* from private to public (state) ownership by the *government*. The opposite of *privatization*.

Neoclassical economics
The dominant approach to economics today. It developed from the free-market ideas of *classical economics* and is based on the concepts of *supply and demand* and individuals making rational choices.

Neoliberalism
An approach to economics and social studies that favors *free trade* and greater *privatization*, along with minimal *government* intervention.

Privatization
Selling state-owned businesses to private investors. The opposite of *nationalization*.

Production
The process of creating *goods* or *services* for sale. Also the total amount produced over a set period.

Productivity
The measure of output by an individual, a *company*, or a whole country. It's usually calculated by dividing the total output over a set period by the number of hours worked, or by the number of workers.

Profit
A firm's total *revenue* minus the total costs.

Protectionism
A policy aimed at protecting a country's economy from foreign competitors, by imposing trade barriers such as *tariffs* or *quotas* on *imports*.

Quota
The limit a country imposes on the number of *goods* imported from another country.

Recession
A period during which the total output of an economy decreases. Severe long-term recession is known as a *depression*.

Revenue
The total amount of money received by a business over a set period. Also the total income of a *government* from taxation and other sources.

Secured loan
A loan that is backed by *assets* belonging to the borrower. If the borrower fails to repay the loan, the lender gets the *assets*. A *mortgage* uses property to secure the loan.

Services
Intangible products, such as hairdressing, transportation, and banking. Services and *goods* are the two key components of economic activity.

Shares
Units of ownership in a *company* that are sold to investors in return for *capital* to develop the business; also called equities.

Socialism
A political and economic system of social equality in which property and the means of *production* are owned and run by the *government* on behalf of the workers, who receive a wage. Less extreme than *communism*, both systems are opposed to *capitalism*.

Stock market
The *market* in which stocks (*shares*) are bought and sold.

Subsidy
Money paid by *government* to keep prices artificially low and protect businesses that would otherwise struggle to compete with *imports*.

Supply
The amount of a product that is available to buy.

Supply and demand
The twin driving forces of the *market* economy. Low *supply* and high *demand* tends to raise prices; high *supply* and low *demand* tends to lower prices.

Surplus
Trade surplus is an excess of *exports* over *imports*. *Government budget* surplus is an excess of *tax revenues* over public spending. The opposite of *deficit*.

Tariff
A *tax* that a country puts on *imports*.

Tax
A charge imposed on firms and individuals by *government*. Its payment is enforced by law.

Index

Note: **bold** page numbers are used to indicate key information on the topic.

A

absolute poverty 110–11
academic economists 8–9
accountants 9
agriculture 36, 42, 43, 93, 105
aid 112–13, 121
Allais, Maurice 148
altcoins 23
analysts 8, 89
applied economics 9
apprenticeships 127
assembly lines 53
ATMs (automated teller machines) 21, 128, 141
austerity policies 91
Austrian school 24, 25, 100

B

bank cards 26, 128
Bank of England 103
banknotes 16–17, 20
bankruptcy 45
banks
    bank accounts 12, 13, 20, 128–9
    deregulation of 90
    failure of 91, 101, 117
    loans 100–1, 116–17, 135, 146
    and money supply 102–3
    savings 142–3
barter 16
bear markets 80

Behavioralist school 24, 88–9
"Big Mac Index" 120
bitcoin 22, 23, 27
Bodin, Jean 148
bonds 45, 80, 82, 101
boom and bust 65, 71
borrowing 100, **116–17**, 120, 134–5
bounded rationality 88
bubbles, economic **72–3**
budgeting 130–5, 146
Buffet, Warren 78, 81, 143
bull markets 80
bureaux de change 18, 19, 140, 141
business cycle 71
businesses
    funding **100–1**, 134
    operation of **50–1**, 52–3
    ownership 48–9

C

capital, raising 45
capital goods 31, 37
capitalism **42–3**, 47, 49
carbon footprints 95
careers 125, 127
cartels 75
cash 12, 20–1, 26, 128–9
Chang, Ha-Joon 148
charities 112, 121
checks 12, 20
Chicago school 24, 118
child labor 35, 95, 120, 137
Classical school 25, 41
climate change 74, **92–3**, 95, 114, 115
cloned bank cards 26

cooperative movement **54–5**, 87
coins 16–17
command economies 47
commission charges 140–1
commodity markets 15, 78
communism 24, 25, 47, 48, 49, 65
company shares 82
comparative advantage 67
competition 46–7, 61, 86
    lack of 74–5
compound interest 143
construction industry 37, 43
consumer cooperatives 55, 87
consumer goods 37
consumer rights/protection 65, 87, 95, 133
consumer society 58–9
consumerism 59
contactless payments 7
corporations, large 49, 61, 69
corruption 113
cost of living 99, 110
costs
    new business start-up 51, 100
    production 50–1
credit cards 7, 12, 20–1, 128, 135, 141
credit rating 134
credit unions 54
creditors 45
crime 23, 26, 27, 65
cryptocurrencies **22–3**
currencies 16–19
    digital 22–3
    pegging 106
    single world currency 27
    travel money 140–1
cyber-security 27

D

debit cards 7, 12, 20–1, 128, 141
debt
    cancellation of 113
    credit card 135
    national 99
    poorer countries 111, 113
debt securities 82, 83
debtors 45
decentralized currencies 22
decision-making **88–9**
default 116–17
deficit 99
demand *see* supply and demand
deposits/depositors 102–3, 117
depression 70
derivatives 78–9, 82, 83
developing countries **104–5**
    and globalization 108–9
    helping 112–13
    poverty and debt **110–11**, 113
development economics 9
digital currency 22–3
direct taxation 77
directors 44, 49, 51
disasters, natural 30, 121
dividends 44
division of labor 52
dollar, US 6, 16, 18, 19, 27, 140, 141
"dotcom" bubble 73

E

Easterlin, Richard 148
economic growth 70, 71, 94, 104

"economic man" 88, 89
economic problem 30–1, 32
economics **6–7**, 25, 26
economies of scale 53
economists 8–9
    directory of 148–51
    forecasts 26
    schools of thought 24–5, 26
electronic transactions **20–1**, 22
emergencies 142, 144–5
emissions, carbon 92, 93, 95, 115
energy 36, **114–15**
Engel, Ernst 148
environmental concerns 34, 71, 75, 77, 92–3, 95, 108
equity 82
ethical concerns **34–5**
the euro 18, 19, 140
European Central Bank 107
European Commission 107
European Union 19
Eurozone 19, 140
exchange rate **18–19**, 140–1
expenditure
    budgeting 130–1
    keeping costs down 132–3
    and savings 129
    unexpected 144–5
exports 43, 66–9, 95
externalities 75

F

factories 42, 48, 53, 137
Fairtrade 34–5
Fama, Eugene 148
fiat money 7, 17
financial analysts 83
financial crisis (2007-8) **90–1**, 116

financial engineering 83, 90
financial instruments 82
Ford, Henry 100
forecasts, economic 80–1, 94
foreign aid 112–13
foreign exchange 19, 78
foreign investment 105
forgery 26
forward contracts 78, 82
fossil fuels 95, 114, 115
fraud 103
free market 25, 46–7, 49, **64–5**, 71, 77, 86–7
    and inequality 118–19
free trade **66–7**
free trade areas 68
free-riding 75
freedom, and equality 119
Friedman, Milton 25, 86, 95, 118
Frisch, Ragnar 148
funds, raising 100
futures market 78–81

G

Galbraith, John Kenneth 17, 49, 57, 148
gambler's fallacy 89
gender gap 136
"Giffen goods" 40
Giffen, Robert 40, 148
global warming
    see climate change
globalization **68–9**, 118
    pros and cons **108–9**
gold 16, 17
gold standard 16
goods and services 14–15, **36–7**
    distribution of 32–3

supply and demand **38–9**, 40
    value of 40–1, 99
government bonds 82
    and failing banks 91, 101, 117
    foreign aid 112–13
    and industry 49
    levels of intervention 25, 33, 47, 64–5, 71, 74, 87, 111
    loans 101
    provision of goods and services 76–7
    and resource management 32
    welfare payments 111, 118, 126, 145
Great Depression 25, 71, 111
Great Recession 91
Greece, bailout/debt crisis 107, 116
greed 86–7
greenhouse gases 92–3, 95, 114
Gross Domestic Product (GDP) 98–9
    per capita 99, 118
    shrinkage in 91

H I

Hayek, Friedrich 24, 25, 100, 118
herd mentality 72, 73
heuristics 89
high quality goods 53
home
    cost of 131, 134
    setting up 145, 147
housing cooperatives 54, 55
human resources 31, 53

Hume, David 32, 148–9
hyperinflation **84–5**
immigration 69
imperialism 104–5
imports 43, 65, 66–9, 94
impulse buying 133
income *see* wages
income tax 77, 95
independent financial advisers 9, 128, 146
indirect taxation 77
Industrial Revolution 24, 42, 43, 58
industrialization 92, 95, 104, 105
industry 42–3
    and the environment **92–3**
    and globalization **108–9**
inequality 87, 110–11, 118–19, 120–1
inflation 84–5
information, disclosure of 74
information technology 43, 53, 61
infrastructure 105, 108, 109, 113
insider trading 74, 87
insurance 145, 146, 147
interest 116, 117, 129, 135, 142–3
international financial institutions **106–7**, 113
International Labor Organization (ILO) 106
International Monetary Fund (IMF) 106, 107, 117
international trade 66–9, 99, 104
internet 43, 53, 147
investors/investments 48, 49, 94, 101, 118, 128, 129, 142–3

J K L

Jevons, William 149
job-share 127
jobs *see* work
joint ownership 48–9
Kahneman, Daniel 72, 88, 89
Keynes, John Maynard 25, 32, 47, 64, 111, 117
Keynsian school 24
Krugman, Paul 67, 117, 149
labor 31, 56–7, 106
    costs 53, 69
    in developing countries 108–9
    division of 52
    management of 51
    movement of 69
labor market 56–7
labor theory of value 41
Laffer, Arthur 77, 149
Lagarde, Christine 149
laissez-faire economy 25, 47, 64, 65
legal tender 17, 18
leisure time 59, 60, 124–5, 131
liberalism 65
limited liability 44
loan agreements 79
loan sharks 120
loans 83, 90, 100–1, 102–3, **116–17**, 129, **134–5**, 145, 146, 147
loss leaders 60
luxury goods 43, 53, 58, 59

M

macroeconomics 9, 27, 111
Madoff, Bernie 103
malpractice, financial 90
Malthus, Thomas 92, 149

man-made resources 31
managers 51, 52, 87, 109, 119
manufactured goods 37, 41, 43, 48, 58
marginal utility 41
market economies 24, 47
    fluctuations in 70–1
markets 7, **14–15**
    failure of **74–5**
    regulation of **64–5**, 71
Marshall, Alfred 24, 25, 38, 149
Marx, Karl 15, 24, 25, 33, 41, 47, 48, 64, 87
Marxist school 24, 41, 64
mass-production 52, 53
mechanization 42–3, 57
medium of exchange 12, 16–19, 20
Menger, Karl 149
microeconomics 9, 27
Mill, John Stuart 42, 149
Minsky, Hyman 82, 149
Minsky moment 82
Mises, Ludwig von 47, 149
mixed economies 49, 65
Modigliani, Franco 149
money
    buying and selling 19
    electronic 20–3
    invention of 6
    supply 102–3
    value of 13, 20
monopolies 46, 74–5
moral hazard 117
mortgages 117, 131, 134, 144, 145
Moyo, Dambiso 113, 150
multinational corporations 69, **108–9**

N O

NASDAQ (National Association of Securities Dealers Automated Quotation) 15
Nash, John Forbes 150
nationalized industries 49
natural resources 30–1, 60, 71, 92, 93, 105, 108
negative income tax 95
Neoclassical school 24, 25
niche markets 61
obsolescence 61
oil 30, 60, 78, 105, 114, 121
online banking services 128
online transactions 21, 22, 59
opportunity cost 41, 124, 125
Ostrom, Elinor 150
outsourcing 53, 69
overdrafts 128–9, 135

P

packages, loan 83, 90
paper money 6–7, 17
Pareto, Vilfredo 150
passwords 147
peer-to-peer payment systems 22
pensions 111, 145
philanthropy 121
Pigou, Arthur 150
PIN (personal identification number) 21, 147
planning ahead 144–5
political economists 8
politics 65
pollution 75, 77, 92–3, 95, 108
Ponzi, Charles 103
population, increase in 30, 31, 71, 92

postindustrial society 43, 60
poverty 104–5, 109, **110–11**
    and foreign aid **112–13**, 121
    poverty trap 111, 113
prices
    and competition 46
    hyperinflation 84–5
    as measurement of worth 13
    and supply and demand 38–9, 78
    and working conditions 35, 120, 137
production costs 50–1, 69
productivity
    competition and 46
    running an efficient business **52–3**
profit 50, 51
    share of 101
promissory notes 20
property, investment in 143
protectionism 67, 68
psychology, and economics 88, 89
public companies **44–5**, 48–9, 100
public expense 75
public goods 74, 75, 76–7
public services 65
Putnam, Robert 150

Q R

quantitative easing 103
Quesnay, François 150
racial equality 137
rare commodities 40
raw materials 36, 50, 51, 53, 69, 108
recession 70, 71, 91
relative poverty 111

renewable energy 115
rent 131, 132, 147
repayments 134–5, 146, 147
research economists 8
resource management 27, 30–1, 60
retail industry 51, 58–9
retirement 145
Ricardo, David 67
risk **80–1**, **82–3**, 117

S

Sachs, Jeffrey 150
salary see wages
sales, revenue from 50–1
sales taxes 77
savings 7, 12, 13, 128, 129, 131, 134, **142–3**, 146
Say, Jean-Baptiste 150
scarcity 30, 38–9
  value 40
Schumpeter, Joseph 47, 150
seasonal work 57
securities **82–3**, 90
security (loan/mortgage) 101, 117, 134, 146
self-employment 127
self-interest 86, 87
Sen, Amartya 150
service sector 36, 37, 43, 53, 59, 60
services see goods and services
shareholders 44, 48–9, 51, 100
shares 15, 44, 48, 49, 51, 72–3, 81, 82, 101, 129
shopping 58–9, 133
short selling 79
silver 16, 17
Simon, Herbert 25, 88–9, 151

skilled labor 56, 57
slave labor 35, 95, 120
small businesses 48, 51
smartcards 21
smartphones 21
Smith, Adam 21, 24, 32, 33, 41, 44, 52, 79, 86, 105
smuggling 94
social mobility 119
socialism 49, 65, 87, 119
South Sea Bubble 73
specialized markets 15
standard of living 70, 71, 98, 99, 104, 111, 118, 121
state-owned enterprises 49, 101
status symbols 59
sterling 6
Stern, Nicholas 74, 151
Stigler, George 151
Stiglitz, Joseph 151
stock markets 15, 45, 72–3, 80, 81, 82
strikes 56
student loans 134
subprime mortgages 90
subsidies, state 65, 75, 101
supply and demand 14, 15, 31, 32–3, **38–9**
  balance of 64, 70
  creating demand 39
  and wages 136
surplus 38–9, 57, 99
sustainable economies 71
sustainable energy sources 115
sustainable growth 109
sweatshops 34, 35, 95, 120, 137

T U

tariffs 67
tax avoidance 77
taxes 65, 76–7, 93, 95, 118
technology 61
Tobin, James 151
trade 7, 24, 106
  ethical **34–5**
  free 66–7
trade unions 56
traders 8, 80–3
transnational corporations 69
travel money **140–1**, 146
trends, market 81
trickle-down theory 119
Tulipomania 72
Tversky, Amos 88, 89
unemployment 57, 111, 126, 145, 147
unit of account 13
United Nations (UN) 110
unskilled labor 109, 136
US Federal Reserve 103, 135
utility 40–1

V W

vacations 140–1, 146
value
  of goods 40–1
  labor theory of 41
  paradox of 40, 41
  storing 7, 12, 13
Varoufakis, Yanis 151
Veblen, Thorstein 59, 151
"virtual" money 21, 27
wage gap 118–19
wages 42, 50, 56
  and budgeting 130–1
  in developing countries 108–9

earning a living **126–7**
rate for the job **136–7**
and work-life balance 124–5
Wall Street Crash 71
Walras, Léon 25, 151
Waring, Marilyn 151
Washington Consensus 107
water 30, 60, 92, 110, 112
wealth
  distribution of 24, 65, **104–5**, 118, 119
  measuring a country's **98–9**, 118, 120
  and poverty 104–5, 110
Webb, Beatrice and Sydney 151
Weber, Max 151
Weimar Germany 84, 85
welfare payments 111, 118, 126, 145
Wieser, Friedrich von 151
wills 145
work 56–7
  dead-end jobs 120
  earning a living 126–7
  work-life balance **124–5**
worker cooperatives 54, 87
worker's rights 56
working conditions 34–5, 56, 65, 95, 108, 120, 137
working hours 60, 124–5
World Bank 106, 110, 113
World Trade Organization (WTO) 106

Y Z

yen, Japanese 18, 19
Zimbabwe, hyperinflation in 85

Acknowledgments

Dorling Kindersley would like to thank Derek Braddon for writing the Introduction (pp. 6–7); John Farndon for writing the In Focus pages; Camilla Hallinan for writing the Glossary; Hazel Beynon for proofreading; and Helen Peters for the index.

The publisher would like to thank the following for their kind permission to reproduce their photographs:

(Key: a–above; b–below/bottom; c–center; f–far; l–left; r–right; t–top)

6 Dreamstime.com: Ilfede (c); Mariasats (cl). 6–7 Dreamstime.com: Wiktor Wojtas (c). 7 Dreamstime.com: Robyn Mackenzie (c); Paul Prescott (cl); Franz Pfluegl (cr). 10 Dreamstime.com: Frenta. 15 Corbis: Ed Eckstein (tr). 16 Corbis: Mark Weiss (bc). 19 Corbis: Photomorgana (tr). 21 Dreamstime.com: Monkey Business Images (br). 25 Dreamstime.com: Pariwatlp (br). 28–29 Dreamstime.com: Bo Li. 30 Corbis: Bojan Brecelj (bc). 32 Corbis: Stefano Bianchetti (br). 37 Dreamstime.com: Zorandim (br). 39 Corbis: Lynn Goldsmith (br). 40 Dreamstime.com: Matyas Rehak (bc). 42 Bridgeman Images: Universal History Archive/UIG (bc). 46 Dreamstime.com: Dave Bredeson (cl). 48 Corbis: AS400 DB (bc). 51 Corbis: Helen King (br). 53 Corbis: (cr). 56 Dreamstime.com: Konstantinos Papaioannou (bc). 62–63 Dreamstime.com: Wiktor Wojtas. 65 Corbis: Mike Segar/Reuters (br). 67 Corbis: AS400 DB (tc). 69 Dreamstime.com: Yanlev (br). 71 Corbis: (br). 75 Dreamstime.com: Tebnad (crb). 77 Dreamstime.com: Tatiana Belova (br). 79 Dreamstime.com: Kasto80 (br). 80 Dreamstime.com: 3quarks (bl). 82 Dreamstime.com: Audiohead (bc). 87 Dreamstime.com: Andrey Burmakin (br). 88 Corbis: Carsten Rehder/dpa (bc). 92 Dreamstime.com: Alexmax (bc). 99 Corbis: Harish Tyagi/Epa (br). 100 Corbis: Hulton-Deutsch Collection (bc). 103 Alamy Images: Zuma Press Inc. (tr). 105 Dreamstime.com: Sergiy Pomogayev (tr). 108 Dreamstime.com: Karnt Thassanaphak (bc). 111 Corbis: Bettmann (br). 113 Dreamstime.com: Komprach Sapanrat (br).116 Dreamstime.com: Joophoek (bc). 118: Corbis: Roger Ressmeyer (bc). 122–123 Dreamstime.com: Alexkalina. 125 Dreamstime.com: Tom Wang (tr). 126 Dreamstime.com: Diego Vito Cervo (bl). 128 Dreamstime.com: Maxuser2 (bc). 131 Dreamstime.com: Nasir1164 (tr). 133 Dreamstime.com: Ljupco Smokovski (tr). 134 Dreamstime.com: Andrey Popov (bc). 139 Dreamstime.com: Rangizzz (br). 141 Dreamstime.com: Matyas Rehak (br). 143 Corbis: Bombzilla (br). 145 Dreamstime.com: Epicstock (br).

Cover images: Front: 123RF.com: Lorna Roberts (tc, cla); Sylverarts (br). Back: 123RF.com: Lorna Roberts (cl); Sylverarts (crb); Dreamstime.com: Sylverarts (tr). iStockphoto.com: Sylverarts (cla). Spine: Dreamstime.com: Sylverarts (t).

All other images © Dorling Kindersley
For further information see: www.dkimages.com